POPPET MAGICK

About the Author

Silver RavenWolf (Pennsylvania) is a nationally recognized leader and elder of Wicca, and her writing has been instrumental in guiding the future of one of the fastest-growing faiths in America today. The author of many books, she has been interviewed by the *New York Times*, *Newsweek*, and the *Wall Street Journal*, and her work has been featured in numerous publications, including *Bust Magazine*, the *Baltimore Sun*, the *St. Petersburg Times*, the *National Review*, *Publishers Weekly*, *Body & Soul Magazine*, and *Teen Lit Magazine*.

Her titles include the bestselling *Solitary Witch*, *Teen Witch*, *To Ride a Silver Broomstick*, *To Stir a Magick Cauldron*, *To Light a Sacred Flame*, *American Folk Magick*, *Angels: Companions in Magick*, *Silver's Spells for Prosperity*, *Silver's Spells for Protection*, *Silver's Spells for Love*, *Halloween*, *HedgeWitch*, and the Witches' Night Out teen fiction series.

LLEWELLYN PUBLICATIONS
WOODBURY, MINNESOTA

POPPET MAGiCK

✶

SILVER RAVENWOLF

PATTERNS,
SPELLS &
FORMULAS FOR
POPPETS,
SPIRIT DOLLS &
MAGICKAL ANIMALS

FIRST EDITION
Second Printing, 2021

Book design by Rebecca Zins
Cover design by Ellen Lawson
All poppets, photos, and illustrations © Silver Ravenwolf
except for photos on pages i, iii, v, xi, 43, 173, and 264 by Ellen Lawson
Fabric swatches and tabletop/burlap/green background image from iStockphoto.com

Llewellyn is a registered trademark of Llewellyn Worldwide Ltd.

Library of Congress Cataloging-In-Publication Data
Names: RavenWolf, Silver, author.
Title: Poppet magick : patterns, spells, and formulas for poppets, spirit
 dolls, and magickal animals / Silver RavenWolf.
Description: First edition. | Woodbury : Llewellyn Worldwide, Ltd., 2018. |
 Includes bibliographical references and index.
Identifiers: LCCN 2017061485 (print) | LCCN 2018007252 (ebook) | ISBN
 9780738756295 (ebook) | ISBN 9780738756158 (alk. paper)
Subjects: LCSH: Magic. | Dolls—Miscellanea.
Classification: LCC BF1621 (ebook) | LCC BF1621 .R375 2018 (print) | DDC
 133.4/3—dc23
LC record available at https://lccn.loc.gov/2017061485

Llewellyn Worldwide Ltd. does not participate in, endorse, or have any authority or responsibility concerning private business transactions between our authors and the public.

All mail addressed to the author is forwarded but the publisher cannot, unless specifically instructed by the author, give out an address or phone number.

Any internet references contained in this work are current at publication time, but the publisher cannot guarantee that a specific location will continue to be maintained. Please refer to the publisher's website for links to authors' websites and other sources.

Llewellyn Publications
A Division of Llewellyn Worldwide Ltd.
2143 Wooddale Drive
Woodbury MN 55125-2989

www.llewellyn.com
Printed in the United States of America

Contents

CONTENTS

3: Basic Poppet Construction
Stitching, Stuffing, and Spellcraft 67

4: Poppet Rituals
Birthing, Naming, Sending, and Deactivating Rituals 103

5: A Plethora of Poppets
Working with Various Mediums 119

CONTENTS

6: Handling Your Spirit Dolls

Taking Care of Your Permanent Poppets 203

7: Poppet Formulas

As I Craft Thee,
So I Wish Thee 213

CONTENTS

CONTENTS

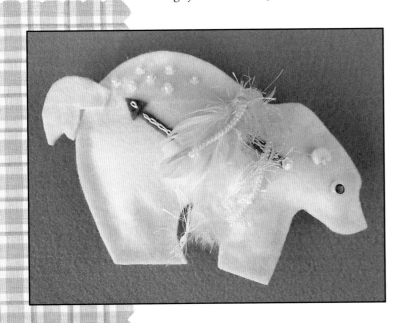

To Nevaeh Elaine
with all my love
no matter where you are
Ama will always be with you

Introduction

My fascination with poppets and effigies began as a child when someone gave me a finger puppet and told me that the puppet had the power to grant wishes. I believed this, and it was so.

Years later, I read an article on creating primitive dolls in a magazine. These interesting creatures are made of muslin, painted, grunged (rubbed with spices, coffee grounds, and wet tea bags, then baked in the oven at 185 degrees), and then dressed with a particular theme, usually country prim, as it is called. I became so enamored with the idea of this do-it-yourself-dolly that I studiously set out to create one. During the process, I realized the amount of energy, care, and time that I put into the doll birthed its own unique magickal pattern, whether I was aware of it or not. When I stuffed the doll, I added empowered sigils, herbs, gemstones, and charms to direct my purpose. After weeks of work, when the doll was finally completed, I sat back and realized that, in its own way, the doll was very much alive.

Interesting.

This feeling brought back the memory of that finger puppet so many years ago that brought me ice cream and pretzels and a ride on a horse. When I foolishly told people about the power of my puppet—you guessed it: the power disappeared, and so did the puppet.

After I created my first primitive doll, I began researching the history of poppets and spirit dolls—how they were used in antiquity and how they are still used today. I made another doll, this time incorporating more magickal applications than before, several based on what I'd learned from my research. Elements of Braucherei and Granny Magick crept into my image-creations as I produced doll after doll. Using my patterns, my daughters even made their own dolls to protect their homes.

For five years I turned from writing to creating—fashioning spirit dolls, ornies, and tucks in various animal shapes and freely sharing those patterns online. You can find many of these patterns for free on my blog at http://www.silverravenwolf.wordpress .com.

Stories about how well the dolls worked for their owners began filtering in. People found the jobs they needed, the harmony they wanted, the healing they desired, and more. I decided to share my techniques so that anyone who wanted to unite magick and spirituality with crafting and art might benefit from what I'd learned.

This book shows you the process of the simple image doll—from a selection of materials and patterns designed by myself to sigils, timing, empowerment, and decommissioning your doll if this falls within its purpose. From a mechanical standpoint, I've provided everything you need to know—from fabric to clay, soap, paper selection and more. Spiritually, I have included incantations and magickal rites in the hope that you find not only the amazing magick in the fulfillment of making something with your own hands, but experience the wondrous power of the magical spirit doll as its energy blesses your life and brings great joy to those you love.

As you read this book, please view it through the lens of humanity rather than through the smoke of your culture or what you think you already know. Allow your mind to be open, and the energies will speak to you in ways you did not think possible. Everyone finds a niche in magick—something that is unique and special to them, something that is super empowering both for themselves and for others. When I make a doll for a person, I throw my whole essence into it—I reach out and touch the spirit-soul of the individual the doll is for, and I may spend days with that open connection until the doll is completed. This spiritual link is a web of pure love, carrying my wishes that the individual be happy, protected, and recover from whatever negative there may be at hand.

Twenty years ago I would have laughed in your face if you told me that I would be a Mistress of Dolls.

And now look at me! Surrounded by poppets, dollies, and spirit animals that have taught me how to send power in loving form to others who are in need. Who woulda thunk?

To me, a doll is an emissary of your creative essence seated in the physical world. So, the question then arises…

What will you send when you make your poppets, dollies, or spirit animals?

My suggestion:

Be loving…be joyful…be filled with the glitter that this life can bring.

Be determined…be artful…be confident!

Before any working, your statements—either aloud or in your mind—should be:

"Yes! This is possible!"

"Yes! The Power is there for me to use, and I'm darned well going to use it!"

"Yes! What I want will be done!"

What's next?

Zap a dolly and do!

The world is anxiously awaiting your creations!

As I stitch thee
So I wish thee

How Old *is* Poppet Magick?

oppets—effigies—dolls—idols…the practice of using doll magick has weathered the rise and fall of politics and religion, surfing the waves from culture to culture, traveling with the ebb and flow of humanity across the globe. Malleable substances such as clay, wax, animal fats, and bread dough were often used in ancient Egyptian magick, enabling the practitioner to form gods, goddesses, people, and animals for purposes of healing, attraction, or banishment (Pinch 1994, 87). Human detritus such as hair, saliva, or nail clippings (called taglocks today) were incorporated into the doll to build a connection between the poppet and the individual the doll represented. Due to the degradation of the material, few cloth dolls exist from antiquity; however, a few have been discovered and preserved from Egyptian tombs. Thanks to the hot, dry sands of Egypt, examples of dolls made of linen and wood with embroidered features and thread hair have been found intact (Edward 1997, 7).

Greek poppets called *Kolossoi* were sometimes used to restrain evil spirits, ghosts, or even a dangerous thoughtform or god intent on wrecking havoc in one's life (Faraone and Obbink 1991). The *defixio* poppet (binding spell doll) consisted of flattened lead in the shape of the familiar gingerbread man. The earliest examples of such defixiones, found in the fifth century BC in Sicily, soon became a favorite vehicle in a wide variety of enchantments. From directing the energy to specifically affect a person, to prayers to gods, to wishes cast upon the worthy (and unworthy), to spells of analogy similar to those we find in Pow-Wow (Braucherei) magick, these effigies turned up all over the Greco-Roman world by the second century AD. This tells us that the practice of using dolls in magick spanned over 700 years and beyond. The flat defixio was inscribed, then rolled or folded and pierced with a bronze or iron nail. Other dolls of the period served a much different, more harmonious purpose—such as the practice of a young woman ritually giving her dolls away on her wedding day.

In Japan the *ningyo kuyo matsuri* (doll-burning festival) is a funeral ceremony for old, unwanted dolls that is still practiced today. This Buddhist practice consists of last rites for loved but unwanted dolls, solidifying the belief that inanimate objects can hold energy gifted to them by the living. Prayers are said, followed by the purification of the dolls, which are offered to the goddess of mercy and then cremated by the priests. It is believed that these dolls not only have memories but may also have souls too. Dates differ on the festival, ranging from June through October. In a 2006 ceremony over 38,000 dolls were ritually burned.[1]

Hinamatsur, which occurs in the spring (March 3), traces its origins to an ancient Japanese custom called *hina nagashi* (doll floating), in which straw hina dolls are set afloat on a boat and sent down a river to the sea, supposedly taking troubles or bad spirits with them. This practice is thought to have begun in the Heian period (794 to 1192) and also continues to this day.

The use of an effigy to perform a spell on someone is documented in African, Native American, and European cultures. Examples of such magickal devices include the European poppet and the *nkisi* or *bocio* of West and Central Africa.[2] From the rag doll found in an AD 300 Roman tomb to the use of vegetables, stones, cloth, sticks, grasses, and wood to create the "dim" of a human, dolls have been used in play, protection, love, healing, or destruction for thousands of years.

---

1   http://www.japantimes.co.jp/life/2006/10/15/to-be-sorted/last-rites-for-the
    -memories-as-beloved-dolls-passaway/#.UuLZaxAo6Uk
2   http:// www.metmuseum.org/art/collection/search/320053

The *Oxford English Dictionary* shows the first mention of the word *poppet* in the medieval world in 1539, the word meaning doll, puppet, or a dim of a form (a replica or shadow in agreement with an animate object), a derivation of a vague reference to a different word in 1413. In 1693 the poppet was mentioned as a vehicle for witches and sorcerers, made of rags and hog bristles, with headless pins in them—the points being outward. Medieval European history, fraught with blood, fear, and religious persecution, shows us rules set forth by the Catholic Church for acceptable magick as shown in the *Malleus Maleficarum* (a treatise on the prosecution of witches and magick in 1487). Unless charms and chants specifically called on Christian elements in a particular way, such practice was considered evil, and one would be put to death for employing them. The poppet was unacceptable. In the *Egyptian Secrets of Albertus Magnus* (a text thought to rest on the works of a twelfth-century European philosopher), we find reference to a spell that details how one is to destroy a curse carried by a puppet (poppet) that is intended to harm livestock: "Take the formula, written upon a scrap of paper, and nail in a secluded spot in the stable" (Magnus, 56).

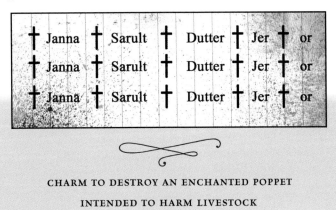

CHARM TO DESTROY AN ENCHANTED POPPET

INTENDED TO HARM LIVESTOCK

Perhaps the most interesting story I found in my research is that of the dream doll. Fashioned with herbs and resins and placed by a burning lamp, the doll is given a mission to perform. The magician even makes a small bed for the doll, commanding it to go forth and empower a queen to produce a son. That son? Alexander the Great (Faraone and Obbink 1991, 181).

Many magickal practitioners think that the well-known Louisiana Voodoo Doll is the combination of a French-style magickal poppet (where the doll represents a person) and the African belief in the bocio (where the doll is a messenger). We find the

European procedure clearly set forth by the writings of Maria de Naglowska inserted into Paschal Beverly Randolph's book *Magia Sexualis* (which is still available today). In the how-to chapter on the laws of correspondence, sympathies, and polarization, the authors discuss the preparation of a "volt"—a poppet that functions with the aid of fluid condensers and astrological timing, both of which I have used in making some of the dolls in this book (Randolph and de Naglowska 1931, 77).

The bocio—the African version of the poppet/spirit doll—is considered a "messenger," not a real person, and traditionally passes energy and information to the spirits, gods, and nature. The bocio itself was not a power—it was a servant/messenger/envoy/carrier that could take the desire of the magickal person (via verbal intent/prayers) to the repository that can affect change (the divine you believe in). This fetish (as in the old sense of the word) was a gateway. The doll opened the door. It unlocked the crossroads where power could be accessed.

Some believe that it was the marriage of European magickal dolls from the French with the bocio ideal (from enslaved peoples brought to this country) that created the American version of the Hoodoo/Voodoo Doll we see today, thus creating a powerful spirit doll in its own right. As a note, those researching the writings of Pascal Beverly Randolph believe that the "volt" and astrological material inserted into *Magia Sexualis* belong entirely to Maria de Naglowska and not Randolph. For more information, you may enjoy reading John Patrick Deveney's work entitled *Paschal Beverly Randolph: A Nineteenth-Century Black American Spiritualist, Rosicrucian, and Sex Magician.*

Claude Lecoutex, author of *The Book of Grimoires: The Secret Grammar of Magic*, also makes mentions of "volts" (magickal dolls) in his research: "The use of figurines, called 'voults,' or of images in evil spells or healing magic was very widespread and still exists in Europe as in other parts of the world." This quote is about a drawn image for use in healing magick (Lecouteux 2002, 94).

From Chaldea through ancient Egypt, from Greece to Rome, and from China to Africa, cultures throughout the world have used poppets to change circumstances, provide protection and defense, bring healing and love, and bind enemies. People and their needs have not changed; thousands of years later we are still making, empowering, and using enchanted dolls. Governments can change, countries can change, technology brings change—but we, of the human condition, still have fears, worries, sickness, compassion, love, and the desire for happiness and security.

And…we still make poppets.

two

Poppet Basics

Intent, Supplies, and Timing

All things—people, places, animals, and nature—are connected. The gatekeeper to opening or closing these connections is the combination of your thought, will, and emotion. This amazing triad of energy that you create can open, close, or move energy along the network that exists among all things. The creation of a poppet accesses that network. Your physical work combined with your mental work enhances and strengthens the connection between your desire and the manifestation. The doll is *never* "just" a doll—it is a vehicle of pure potential. When you make a poppet or spirit doll, you are riding the network of creation.

Although many people think that a poppet represents a specific person (and it can), poppets also can be used to access a plethora of energies—from information gathering, clarity, healing, compassion, courage, and overcoming obstacles to attracting prosperity and much more. These images are often called spirit dolls. Dolls can represent the spirit of an inanimate object, such as a house, a car, or a piece of property. They can also be associated with nature, your garden, or your pets. With a poppet or spirit doll (or in any other magickal endeavor), if you think it, you create it. A poppet or spirit doll *becomes* the bond (the marriage) of the mental and physical.

All poppets/spirit dolls will work if:

- your intent is clear

- you have established a clear connection to the network of creation

The Purpose of Your Poppet

The fashioning of any poppet or doll figure begins with your intent. What specifically is the doll for? Do you want to make a doll to represent your sister and place healing herbs and sigils within it or do you want to fashion a poppet to represent the disease that has plagued her? Will your spirit doll be a messenger? A friend to carry around with you? A key to something you need? Poppets fall under two main categories: effigies of people or representations of a particular form of energy activity (banishment, serenity, grief recovery, happiness, etc.).

From the choice of effigy or energy, we move into the concept of attracting or repelling. Are you looking for love or do you need financial security? Do you desire to banish debt or remove the damage gossip has caused in your life? Once we have determined whether we want to pull something toward us or push something away, we move on to the choice of the life of the poppet.

If you are working for good luck in the home, you may wish to create a poppet that will last at least a year or more. However, if you are trying to banish a particular disease, you may wish to destroy the poppet in a timely manner—anywhere from immediately upon empowerment in ceremony to three days later. Poppets of this nature are not usually kept beyond that time as the negativity can take hold within the life of the practitioner and become stuck, making the problem worse than before.

These three concepts constitute the formulation of your basic intent and the life purpose of your poppet or spirit doll:

- effigy versus energy

- attraction versus banishment

- long term versus short term

Your choices within these categories guide your steps throughout the process, from choosing the materials, colors, embellishments, sigils, timing, and ceremonial applications (in which the poppet will be empowered) to deciding whether you will dismantle or destroy the doll upon completion of your work.

For example, if the poppet/spirit doll will be used to promote your sister's healing, you may not want to take it apart immediately (or at all, depending upon your purpose). The same might be true for a doll that represents attracting protective energies, money, or good fortune to the household; this type of poppet can be kept for years if you like, re-empowering it on a special day once a month or perhaps once a year. If the doll stands for your sister's disease, your personal debt, or someone who has brought negativity into your life, then it most likely will be burned or in some way dismantled upon performing your magickal working—if not immediately, then shortly after that.

Your intent, then, is the pivotal aspect of the poppet from which all other choices will be made. The clearer your intent, the more powerful the doll. The moment you settle on that intent in your mind is when the magick begins. I've found it extremely helpful to write out my intent for the doll, being very specific about what I want to come to pass. Write this statement out several times until the words precisely reflect the need. Keep this written statement with your supplies for the doll. You can use it when writing a petition to put in the doll, at the end of the doll's birthing ceremony, and in any spellwork done with the doll. That way, your intent throughout the process will stay in sync at every stage of development.

When you make a poppet or spirit doll, you are surfing the network of energy creation: every doll becomes a memory of a moment in time that blends your materials, your emotions, your intent, and your will into a desired result. Every doll, then, is completely individual and unique.

Choosing a Medium

Fabric, clay, wax, sticks, vegetables, mud, tin, paper, cork, wood, snow, stone, cardboard—what medium speaks to you? Are you going for speed? (Paper!) Simplicity? (A potato!) Perhaps you are comfortable working with wood, so a poppet from that material would suit you just fine. How much time do you have to make this poppet? A few minutes (draw it in the dirt), about an hour or two (a clay poppet), or is there a large block of time at your leisure (felt or cotton with embellishments)?

Your emotions play a big part in medium choice—what makes you feel empowered, strong, confident? What medium gives you that knowing experience when you pick it up and begin to make your poppet? Can you feel the energy immediately zing through your fingers? Do you feel really good about what you are doing as you work with the medium? Are you comfortable with the material? Does it frustrate you or does the creation flow smoothly? I like to work with fabric for long-term poppets, particularly those for healing, dreaming, and spirituality. For banishing I prefer clay, mud, or snow. I also use potatoes because they easily rot. This book contains instructions for fabric, paper, and clay—although many of the sections, such as cleansing your supplies and birthing your poppet, as well as the formulas, will lend themselves well to almost any medium you choose.

Poppet Construction Guide

I use the following steps when constructing a poppet:

1. Set the intent. Perform the Rite of the Golden Needle now or at any time during the construction process or not at all—your choice.

2. Consider magickal timing.

3. Determine if the poppet will be a temporary vehicle of magick or a permanent one.

4. Do you want a poppet as in the traditional human figure, a spirit doll (which has more leeway in body choice), or a magickal animal? Which form do you think will work best for your desire? Choose the medium (cloth, paper, clay, etc.) and associated pattern.

5. Decide if this poppet will be decommissioned (ritually taken apart after use) or left intact.

6. Choose what items might be helpful in matching the intent (a special charm, certain herbs, etc.).

7. Gather supplies matching the intent. If the poppet represents a specific person, you will need a taglock, or an item that "locks on" to a person and provides an energy conduit, such as hair, fingernail clippings, a piece of unwashed clothing they have worn, dirt they have walked on, or even spit. You can also write their name on a piece of paper nine times, burn the paper, and use the ashes. I have used an individual's phone number, a discarded drinking straw, and scrapings of wood from a chair where they have rested for many hours. There is no end to your creativity when it comes to finding a suitable taglock! Think of a taglock like a GPS device or like the talons of a bird sinking into flesh and locking on for dear life. Modern or gothic, you choose the analogy.

8. Cleanse and bless all supplies.

9. Construct the poppet.

10. Stuff the poppet, adding magickal herbs, physical charms, and a taglock (see step 7). Also include the individual's name, birthdate (if you have it), sigils, or other items.

11. Stitch shut or otherwise close the poppet.

12. Add any outside embellishments (beads, creative stitching or painting, physical charms, taglock, name, sigils, or other items).

13. Place poppet in the birthing pot.

14. Birth and name the poppet.

15. Use the poppet in spellwork, meditation, ritual, or ceremony.

There is only one area in which I sometimes deviate: when I cleanse and bless the special items that will embellish or be included in the poppet. There are occasions when I have the poppet constructed but wish to take a trip to find something special to add to what I already have. I may wait to choose a particular sigil or construct a sigil with a particular astrological influence. Sometimes I take a Spirit Walk—a walk outside with the specific intent of observing—letting divinity show me what items I should put in the poppet. The cleansing and blessing of these items are done separately, as I obtain or construct them.

FELT BEADED DIVINATION SPIRIT DOLL
WITH HAND-PAINTED FACE

The Rite of the Golden Needle
A mini ritual of balance for any crafter

I developed the Rite of the Golden Needle for the preparation of self before beginning any spirit doll work, and it can be easily adjusted for any creative work that you do. It is a process of calling balance into the body, mind, and spirit with deep breathing, honoring the spirit of "all that is," and acknowledging that you are connected to everything. The rite is more mental than physical, although I do use the following on a regular basis:

- sea salt

- a candle—color matching my intent or the color of the day I was born (This candle is dressed with oil of the intent and liquid universal fluid condenser. Sometimes I use two candles—one for myself and one for my intent. I use purple a great deal with other colors as it is a power pusher, good for boosting protection, uncrossing, and righting wrongs.)

- a golden needle

- blessed water (water you have prayed over)

- incense (optional)

To perform the Rite of the Golden Needle, sit quietly. Light incense if you are using it. Breathe deeply several times. Place the sea salt, the unlit candle, and the blessed water anywhere in front of you. Place a golden needle directly in front of you, preferably in the center of the objects. View this ceremony as a very holy activity—something that requires honor within the self.

Continue to breathe deeply, emptying your mind of all thoughts. I realize this is difficult. Tell yourself it is okay to slow down and chill for just a moment. The world will not explode and go away while you do this—and frankly, if it did, then this wouldn't matter anyway, would it?

Right now it is just you, this place, this time, and "all that is." Allow yourself to connect with "the all" and accept that this connection exists with all people, animals, plants, etc. Enjoy this vibrant, light-filled energy. Don't just think it; FEEL it. You may suddenly find yourself in a web of light—yes, that is perfectly fine.

Rub the salt between the palms of your hands and say: "With this salt, I cleanse all negativity and unclean thoughts from my body, mind, and spirit." Throw the salt over your left shoulder and say: "Only the good remains."

Sprinkle the water over both palms of your hands. Say: "With this water, I bless my body, mind, and spirit so that I may create healing, good fortune, joy, and grace for myself and my family." (You can alter these words as you see fit.) Touch your third eye (the middle of your forehead) with the water. Touch your heart chakra with the water. Take a deep breath and "pull in" divinity.

Light the candle, saying: "I light this candle, bringing the light of wisdom and love into my body, mind, and soul."

Pass the light over the golden needle three times, saying: "As this candle burns, this light of peace, wisdom, and harmony will permeate all of my work."

Pick up the golden needle and hold it in your dominate hand. Blow three times on the needle, saying: "As I stitch thee, so I wish thee. What I desire will come to pass. So be it!"

Allow the candle to continually burn. It is okay to put it out when you stop working on your project and relight it again later. Keep the needle with you or allow it to stay in the center of your altar (perhaps the needle itself need not be used, but the essence of the magick it represents is required).

You can finish by drawing an equal-armed cross over the working or you can add my sea of potential sequence here, which can be found in my book *The Witching Hour*.

Magickal Timing
Knowing when to construct or birth your poppet

There are several methods for magickal timing, including moon quarters, moon phases, the moon in the signs, the days of the week, the planetary hours, and the mansions of the moon. Where some practitioners are eager to work with magickal timing, incorporating all of the above, others are not. In this book we'll cover the moon quarters. Should you like to investigate more extended magickal astrological information, please see my book *The Witching Hour*, where I have provided fine-tuned planetary information.

The most basic timing is what is often used in Braucherei magick: the divisions of the day. Dawn for beginnings and birth of all kinds. Noon for power, motivation, success, and strength (or astrologically when the sun hits its zenith for your area). Twilight for confusion, stealth, glamouries, and general banishment. This rural/agricultural-type (but extremely effective) timing can be added to that of the quarters of the moon, phases, planetary hours, etc., or simply used by itself.

Moon Quarters: Waxing and Waning Energies

The best way to work with the quarters of the moon is by following an almanac or calendar with the quarters listed, arranging your work to match the energies available through the power of the moon. Calendars can be purchased in paper form, such as *Llewellyn's Planetary Guide*, viewed on the internet, or downloaded via an app to your phone, notebook, or iPad. Most of these calendars also include the moon in the signs, and some provide planetary hour information. Always remember that the moon doesn't make people do things—rather, it reflects the energies available that you can use to enhance your working.

The New Moon and First Quarter

The new moon is when the sun and the moon are astrologically conjunct (together) in the same sign. This means that both the power of the sun and moon are doubled, each playing off the other—will and emotion combined for a successful working. As there are twelve signs of the zodiac, there are twelve separate new moon types. The consensus of new moon energy is that it is a time to get things started, whether you are beginning a business, buying a home, or learning a new skill. The new moon is the time of birthing all ventures. The correspondences listed below are tailored to possible poppet usage.

Aries New Moon: Aggression, beginnings, inspiration, men and male energy, defense of the home and family, and victory. Perfect for seven-day poppets wherein you will do a spell or ritual each day for seven days focusing on the poppet and your intent. Excellent for creating a motivation poppet. I made Taco Cat (a grunged, painted spirit doll) during an Aries new moon and filled him with a variety of motivational trinkets, herbs, and spices, including cinnamon, ginger, galangal, carnelian gemstone, and ghost peppers. Then I rubbed taco spices all over his body and baked him in the oven. Taco Cat helped me quit smoking cold turkey—no aids or crutches—and I did not backslide (I smoked for thirty years).

I have also used him in other personal motivational magick. (You can see more pictures of Taco Cat by visiting my Facebook page or viewing my Instagram.) I even use his picture as the wallpaper for my phone and computer (see photo at right). He reminds me to never give up and never give in. Ruled by Mars. Element of fire.

Taurus New Moon: Stability, security, and material comfort. Good for seven-day rituals for the protection of home and property (the Cancer moon is also good for this) and for peace in the home. Prosperity magick, particularly when Venus, the sun, or Mercury is well aspected. Feed your house spirit dolly (the doll that brings food, good fortune, and joy into your home). Ruled by Venus. Element of earth.

Gemini New Moon: Communication, intelligence, charging poppets of all kinds, capturing thieves. Good to begin seven-day rituals wherein communication is the key to your success. A good moon to "send" your dolls of all kinds. As most of our money these days is tied to electronics, Mercury has become a "go-to" for prosperity magick, particularly if your money comes to you via the banking system, the internet, data transfer, etc. Ruled by Mercury. Element of air.

Cancer New Moon: Protection, family, healing, women's issues, advancement in your job or career that will directly affect home life, domination, compelling and controlling. Ruled by moon. Element of water.

Leo New Moon: Success, generosity, children, passion, increasing your talent, building your knowledge in a particular skill, lawsuit spells, promotional work, gaining money from a specific person (add Jezebel root), self-confidence. Ruled by sun. Element of fire.

Virgo New Moon: Solutions, healing people and animals, detail, planning, organizing, open the pathway to bring money into the home—can also be used for commanding and compelling work. Ruled by Mercury. Element of earth.

Libra New Moon: Stabilization of the self, create deity dolls, marriage, partnership, negotiations, teamwork, cooperation, asking for help in difficult times, bringing beauty into any situation or place. Ruled by Venus. Element of air.

Scorpio New Moon: Sex, money from others, radical change, creativity of all kinds, unearthing information, genealogy, discovering secrets, money spells for your own business or capital gain. Ruled by Mars (classical) and Pluto (modern). Element of water.

Sagittarius New Moon: Winning, achievement, justice, general self-improvement, good luck, legal issues, humor and joy dolls for healing and general happiness. Ruled by Jupiter. Element of fire.

Capricorn New Moon: Structure, senior citizens, authority, recognition, strategy, organization, guidelines, bringing in material necessities, reward, money owed you, food and lodging for the family, help from someone wiser than yourself, reward for your hard work, binding, holding something temporarily. Ruled by Saturn. Element of earth.

Aquarius New Moon: Innovation, freedom, technology, social groups, psychic pursuits, astrology, uncovering mental health issues. The perfect moon to make and utilize a shopping buddy spirit doll to find all the great deals and protect yourself from being cheated. A super time to make such a doll would be either the Aquarius new moon, or when the sun is in Aquarius and the moon is in Virgo, or when the sun is in Virgo and the moon is in Aquarius. Ruled by Saturn (classical) and Uranus (modern). Element of air.

Pisces New Moon: Divination, dreaming, goals, spirituality, wisdom, throw an enemy off track, confuse the enemy, purification, visionary work of all kinds, spirit animal preparation, seeing the big picture. Ruled by Jupiter (classical) and Neptune (modern). Element of water.

The six days after the new moon are called first quarter, where the momentum of the new moon energy is at its strongest. During this time the moon will move out of the sun's sign and travel into the next sign or two (depending on its momentum). What sign it moves to can tell you how your new moon work will play out—will it be slow or fast, like a shooting star? For example, if the new moon is in Pisces and you have done visionary work that is associated with that sign, then as the moon moves into Aries the Pisces vision you worked on will have a decidedly motivational and fiery flare. Your signal that your magick is working will most likely be in Aries energy form. This is one way to tell if your spell, ritual, or rite is on the right track and will be successful. You will see progress on your original issue associated with the next sign's energy.

The Second Quarter Moon

The second quarter moon is actually a square between the sun and the moon. This is a time when challenges can be overcome to move forward or when friction is applied in a positive way to accomplish a goal. This is the building cycle when you add to a continuing project or expend renewed effort into your creation. Again, the moon continues to move quickly through the astrological signs, giving you an idea how to employ your ideas.

The period from the new moon through the second quarter moon is called waxing. The waxing moon (in general) is good for starting all sorts of things, planting, leaving on a trip, bringing things out into the open, and enjoying new experiences, ideas, places, and people. It is a time of summoning, action, gathering, growing, and binding.

Full Moon and Third Quarter

The full moon is in opposition between the sun and the moon with the earth in the middle in the third quarter. Yet, opposition doesn't mean the energies cannot be compromised—quite the opposite: the energies put together from the opposing signs actually create a dynamic whole. That which is opposing drops away or transmutes (depending on the situation), and that which empowers or remains joins together. Think of yin and yang or the God and Goddess, where two separate energies meld to create a third, more powerful energy than either of the two if they stood alone. It is up to you to pull both energies together and create the harvest of your desires. The two astrological signs in a full moon always pair together, meaning in the twelve-month cycle you will always have six pairs. However, in one instance the sun will be in one sign and the moon will be in the opposite, and the next time the same signs pair, the moon will be in the place of the sun and the sun will be in the opposite sign. If this sounds like gibberish, here are the six pairs:

Aries: Libra (fire and air)

Taurus: Scorpio (earth and water)

Gemini: Sagittarius (air and fire)

Cancer: Capricorn (water and earth)

Leo: Aquarius (fire and air)

Virgo: Pisces (earth and water)

For example, when the sun is in Aries, the full moon will be in Libra. When the sun is in Libra, the full moon will be in Aries. The elements of the pairs give you a structure to work with—for example, if the next full moon is in Cancer, then the sun would be in Capricorn. Your working could include water (associated with Cancer) and earth (associated with Capricorn). This is great timing for a poppet constructed to affect the structure of the home or a poppet made for a senior citizen or a poppet for changing circumstances with an authority figure who is affecting your root welfare.

Third Quarter Moon: Now is a time of banishing, of putting to rest, of closing off, of cleaning out, and of organizing, ditching what is harmful, and locking things up that you want to protect. Most compelling, commanding, confusion, or controlling work is done during this time, although some practitioners opt for the beginning of the fourth quarter moon, not the end. A great time to work on healing chronic disorders and small medical problems like skin irritations, warts, etc. Difficulties such as gossip, lying, and catching thieves fall under the energy of the third quarter moon. Once again, the moon is square the sun, urging you to move into action.

Fourth Quarter Moon: There's a debate among magickal practitioners on what should or should not be done during the fourth quarter moon. Some feel that this week is a time of rest and that no magick should be performed, particularly the day before the new moon. Others take the stance that all major banishings should be done at this time, including breaking bad habits, removing cancer, and turning back criminal evil. In Braucherei it was a time of practicality—of thoroughly washing and sweeping floors, cleansing body and mind, grooming animals, cleaning food-related surfaces to ensure good health, and turning back evil of all kinds. Some feel that it is okay to use the fourth quarter the first few days of the cycle and then rest the remaining time until the new moon. I often burn release dolls at this time.

The third and fourth quarter moons are considered the waning moon. This is a good time for decreasing anything, planting below-the-ground crops, working on things that should stay secret, sending away bad energy, returning negative energy to the person who sent it, coming back from a trip, letting go of just about anything, donating goods and services, dieting, and harvesting.

Remember that making a poppet does not require perfect magickal timing and does not overshadow your intuition—timing is a tool that you can use to enhance your intent, drawing on those energies to fine-tune your working.

Magick and Color

Color figures strongly in a variety of magickal disciplines. Psychologically, color can affect our emotions, heightening or worsening the way we feel. Color affects a magickal operation on two levels: its specific vibrational pattern and how it affects not only the practitioner but the recipient of the doll as well (if the poppet is a gift). The following list of colors is only a general guideline for use; your intuition will guide you on the right color for any poppet, spirit doll, or enchanted animal. A single color can be chosen or a triad of hues or colors mixed in a particular pattern. You may wish to do a meditation and allow Spirit to show you the correct color for the individual. If you are unsure, collect colored stones or paint colored disks and keep them in a sacred pouch. Like a divinatory tool, connect with the individual who needs the doll, take a deep breath, and then ask what colors would suit that person at this time. Draw one or three colors from the bag, indicating that the first color is the primary theme and the second colors supporting.

White or Cream: Purity, spirituality, cleansing, divinity, peace, healing, protection, cure illness, stop libel and slander, and unconditional love. Associated with all colors and the five elements (earth, air, fire, water, and spirit). White is the go-to color for anything. Don't worry if you don't have other colors; white will always work. I prefer to use muslin fabric for most of my stuffed dolls, which is cream in color.

Red: Action, love, lust, passion, domination, speed, strength, courage, athletics, speedy recovery, motivation, war, attack, sports, and leadership. Associated with the planet Mars, Tuesday, and the fire element. A red doll carries a great deal of power; if you think it is too much, mitigate with embellishments of other colors. Dragon's blood resin mixed with yohimbe herb and ground red peppers ramp up the power of any red doll. For love, try using a combination of white, red, and pink. Add orange if there are problems in a current relationship or silver if there is a communication issue.

Yellow: Success, winning, attraction, generosity, money and prosperity, determination, kindness, stamina, loyalty, joy, self-confidence, persuasion, happiness, understanding, and focus. Use white or yellow for dollies with purple embellishments to facilitate an uncrossing. A mixture of marigold, sunflower petals, and golden sand lends power to a yellow poppet. For real estate endeavors, try using yellow, brown, and green in your design and stuff the poppet with dirt from the property you are trying to buy or sell. Associated with the sun, Sunday, and the fire element.

Orange: Opportunity, the ability to adapt, open the way to success, enhance romance, creativity, personal power, rein in a situation that has gotten out of control, and business luck. Dried orange peel and mistletoe push commanding energy into a poppet. Associated with Jupiter, Thursday, and the fire element.

Green: Prosperity, growth, money, general good luck, fertility, gain, increase, wealth, physical comfort, self-love, recuperation. To attract wealth, use a green and gold poppet (or a green poppet stitched with golden thread) stuffed with rue (the great attractor), a magnet, pumpkin seeds, snakeroot, and golden sand. Associated with Jupiter or Venus, Thursday or Friday, and the earth element.

Blue: Protection, harmony, healing for women and children, sympathy, compassion, devotion, understanding, mental pursuits, commanding, the safety of hearth and home. Use blue and white dollies for harmony within the home. If you are having a problem with your spouse or partner, make a dolly of blue and orange—stitch with silver thread and add hazel leaves and dried basil to the poppet. Associated with the moon and Mercury, Monday and Wednesday, and the water and air elements.

Purple: Spirituality, higher mind, psychic pursuits, dreams, spiritual communication, career ambition, protection against ghosts and astral nasties, expansion of business and wealth. Use a combination of purple and orange for winning legal battles or relief from injustice or false accusations. Purple is also associated with protection of the innocent. Associated with Jupiter, Thursday, and the water and air elements.

Pink: Friendship, partnership, harmony among humans, healing, affection, compassion, and kindness. In the medical community pink is associated with good health, therefore making a dolly for healing that is pink or has pink embellishments pulls the group mind ideal of "healthy" into the image. Be sure to add basil herb if there is an obstacle in your love life! Sometimes associated with Venus, Friday, and the air element.

Brown: Miracles, fertility, hidden wealth or hidden information, secrets, confusing an enemy. Excellent for bringing an object into manifestation—from the mind to the physical. Also good for garden magick poppets (blessing the garden and plant spirits). Brown can help to materialize any desire, so adding brown to just about any design is a magickal boost. Patchouli ramps up the vibration of brown. Associated with Saturn, Saturday (rewards or limits), and the element of earth.

Black: Return, the void where all things manifest, protection, reversing, transformation, chaos, karma to bear, transformation. Associated with Pluto or Saturn, Saturday, and the element of earth.

Gray: Secrets, illusion, glamour, neutrality, fog. Use clove and gray to compel an enemy to see only what you wish. Skullcap herb is thought to control the thoughts of others, particularly men. Snakeroot is good for quietly banishing unwanted people; roll in naturally shed snakeskin for more power. Associated with Neptune, Wednesday or Saturday, and the element of water.

Poppet Patterns for Cloth and Paper

The 36 patterns included in this book can be employed for cutting and sewing using felt, cotton cloth, or as a guide for creating paper poppets. To resize patterns, scan the original with computer equipment and then resize using an art or photography program. The patterns are:

The Standard Gingerbread-Style Poppet, Male and Female Versions: This pattern is very easy to cut out, stuff, and sew. Reduce the patterns to use in paper magick, conjuring bags, roll into amulets or talismans, or cut and sew with felt like a pin or a broach.

The Intermediate Male and Female Poppet: A different style of poppet that requires more careful cutting. This pattern is recommended for felt.

The Basic Triangle: Perfect for manifestation work.

The Basic Rectangle: Easy to carry and stuff. You can animate these designs with faces and appendages or use them as sachets or conjuring bags.

No Arms Spirit Poppet: Arms can be added by inserting a stick if you like, or you can make the poppet without arms. This one is most like the African bocio. Objects can be wrapped with twine or string on the outside so that the doll can "carry" the energy/message to where you need it to go. Certain Native American tribes also wrap sacred objects on the outside of their spirit animal dolls. You can also paint the arms and hair on this type of doll. I love this simple design because it works so well for a variety of decorating styles and creative ideas. Plant spirits seem to particularly like this shape.

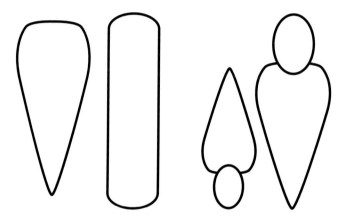

Goddess Poppet: For petitions to female divinity—a particular goddess or the type of energy you need from divinity, such as healing or safe childbirth. There are two patterns, one for felt and paper and one specifically for fabric.

Wings and No Arms Little Spirit Poppet: Perfect for energy work: good luck, jinx removal, protection, etc. Can be affixed easily to a keychain or carried in the pocket. Angel wings are included that can be sized and used on any poppet.

Three-Headed Poppet: Primarily designed for situations where you are having a problem with a group of people or wish to employ triple energies geared with the same focus. This pattern can be adapted into two forms—just the heads or the heads with a body. Once constructed, the pattern can be left as is or you can ritually sever the three heads and body to separate the group energy. Good for banishing disease where there are several symptoms or where there is more than one disease attacking the body.

Spirit Dolly Poppets: These three patterns are great shelf-sitters. Because of their structure, they take dried bean stuffing or plastic pellet stuffing well. Also, because they are wider, they are easier to embellish.

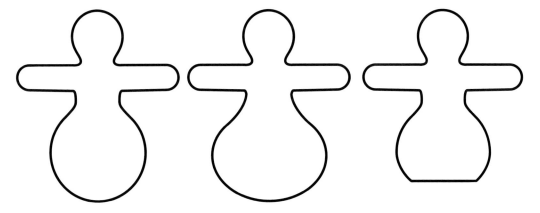

Salt Dolly-Do: This pattern was created so that you can fill the doll with herbs, salt, etc., and hang the hat over a belt or cord so that you can carry her with you to ward off negativity, illness, etc.

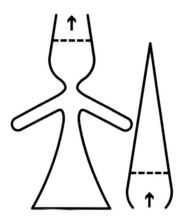

Susie Salt Healer's Tool: The top of the head is left open on this doll for ease in changing or renewing the contents. Use replaceable cord, twine, or ribbon to close the doll's head.

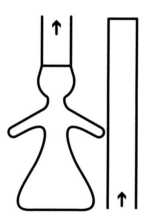

Skull & Crossbones: Created for any type of ancestral work. These are considered "ornies" or "shelf-sitters" and are usually placed in a basket or cauldron.

Gnome: What book on doll and animal spirits wouldn't be complete without a gnome pattern? This design lends itself very well to colorful felt.

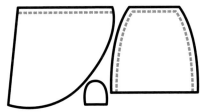

Witch and Chakra Oppits: Flat images that can be used as bookmarks, hanging decorations, or tucked inside dresser drawers or other tight spaces. Mine hang from my ritual staff. The instructions for these designs include a heavy fabric stabilizer.

Animal Patterns: The swan, gargoyle, crow, mojo cat, painted pony, prosperity pig, bat, medicine bear, chakra fish, bunny, restful sleep sheep, and so on (not all patterns are represented on this page)—these animal spirit patterns can be used for a variety of purposes, from connecting to the essence of the animals to working with their spiritual attributes. Their focus is entirely up to you.

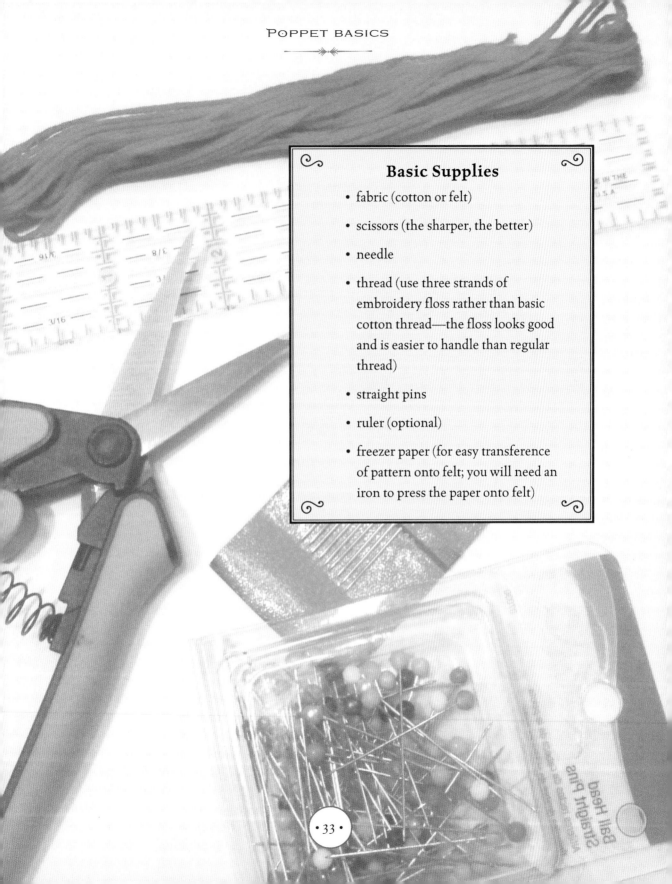

Basic Supplies

- fabric (cotton or felt)

- scissors (the sharper, the better)

- needle

- thread (use three strands of embroidery floss rather than basic cotton thread—the floss looks good and is easier to handle than regular thread)

- straight pins

- ruler (optional)

- freezer paper (for easy transference of pattern onto felt; you will need an iron to press the paper onto felt)

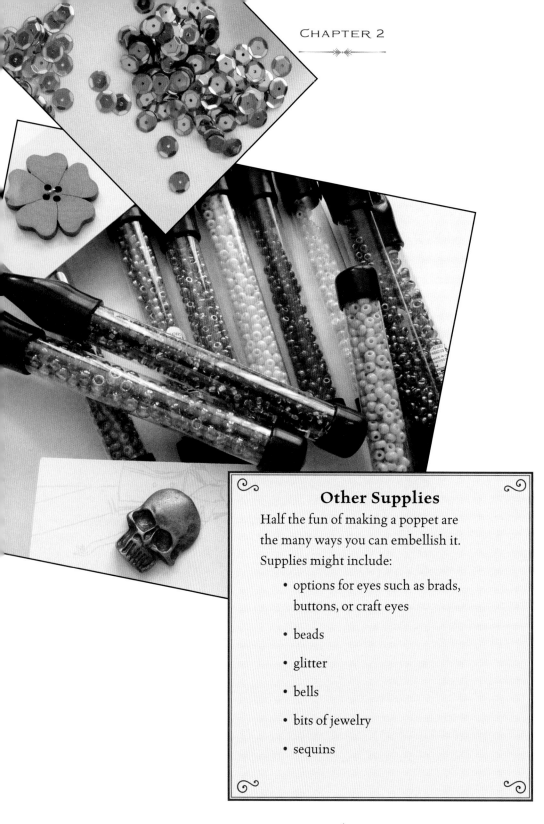

Other Supplies

Half the fun of making a poppet are the many ways you can embellish it. Supplies might include:

- options for eyes such as brads, buttons, or craft eyes

- beads

- glitter

- bells

- bits of jewelry

- sequins

Handpainted faces can be achieved by cutting a piece of muslin to fit the shape of the head, painting the cloth with clear gesso (so the face won't "bleed"), and then painting the face on the treated muslin with acrylic paints. You can also use an acrylic sealer to paint over the face after it has dried to protect the finished design from dirt or water damage. Affix the finished face with Liquid Stitch, glue, or sewing around the edges.

If your doll is made of plain cotton or muslin, you won't need to cut out the face shape—you can paint directly on the doll.

HANDPAINTING THE FACE: FROM LEFT, APPLY GESSO, PAINT FACE (I USE A 00 BRUSH FOR CLEAR LINES), THEN AFFIX FACE TO POPPET

USE A RUBBER STAMPING TECHNIQUE TO ADD
AN UNUSUAL DESIGN TO A MUSLIN POPPET

The Choice of Fabric

Poppets can be made of many materials, such as paper, fabric, wax, wood, or metal, or a combination of a variety of materials. These instructions concentrate primarily on fabric dolls; however, you can easily make adjustments for other materials. Felt is an excellent choice for the long-term poppet—particularly those for protection, good fortune, success, and general good health. With a pair of sharp scissors, felt can be cut quickly, doesn't fray, and is easily stitched either by hand or by machine. A felt poppet doesn't require seam allowances, as the stitching is done on the right side of the fabric, using either the whip stitch, running stitch, blanket stitch, or a sewing machine.

With today's ecofriendly brands and a variety of colors, poppets made of felt are both serviceable and incredibly unique and crafty! The only drawback to felt is that the material doesn't burn well, so if your poppet is of a temporary nature in which you plan a ritual burning, you may have a problem. There is nothing like firing up the cauldron, speaking words of power, laying on the flame, and…nothing. The poppet continues to stare at you, almost a leer, and maybe it smolders or playfully sizzles…but nothing more. Unless you douse it with a fire accelerator, your magick dissolves while your frustration soars—and the stink of smoldering felt is horrendous.

Flannel, printed cotton, and muslin are great choices for temporary poppets—particularly those you plan to burn—or for those poppets where primarily machine stitching is desired or when you truly desire an ultra-primitive look to a more permanent poppet. Easily sewn, the only drawback may be the material fraying at the seams, which can lead to problems if you overstuff the doll. Top stitching by hand can be done with a running stitch; however, you may prefer to sew the poppet's right sides together, leave an opening, and turn the poppet right-side out, which will render a finished seam on the outside. The patterns can be enlarged to provide a seam allowance if you so desire. Use a smaller rendition for felt work and a larger one for cotton fabrics where you desire an inside seam of ¼ inch.

The example shown here is the triangular poppet pattern drawn with a pencil on unbleached muslin. I wanted this poppet to be fairly primitive, so I used a ruler to mark an opening on both sides of the shoulders. When stitching with a machine, I left both areas open. Then I trimmed the seams, clipped the curves, and turned the poppet right-side out using one of the shoulder openings. Notice I left a good amount of material around the open seams so that I could easily fold the material inward once the doll is right-side out.

I OFTEN DRAW THE POPPETS DIRECTLY ONTO MUSLIN PIECES WITH A PENCIL, USING A RULER TO MARK THE OPENING ON BOTH SIDES OF THE DOLL WHERE THE STICK FOR THE ARMS WILL BE PLACED; YOU CAN ALSO PIN THE PATTERN DIRECTLY ON THE MUSLIN AND STITCH NEXT TO THE PAPER

How to Grunge Fabric

Distressed material works extremely well for a variety of magickal projects—from sachet squares to spirit dolls, altar ornaments and coverings, basket ornies, conjuring bags, and even primitive jewelry! Squares of grunged material make great softly scented petition squares that can be carried with you, used in art forms, or burned in the ritual cauldron.

This section covers two types of grunge techniques in an effort to show you how to infuse an already fun craft with loads of enchantment. The first technique only takes a few minutes to do; the remainder of the time the item spends in the oven so you can do something else while your material is perfectly grunging itself! The second technique does take longer, but the result is definitely worth it, particularly if you like the leather look without the leather. This form of grunge makes great cloth squares for petitions.

Why Grunge Material?

In the crafty world, grunging material falls under the category of primitive or country primitive. The techniques produce material that looks old or antique and emits a lingering, pleasant aroma due to the coffee and spices used in the application. These grunging formulas set your magickal project in motion simply by their own correspondences. Although you can grunge almost any type of cotton material, most crafters start with economical muslin, which in my area of the country is $1.99 to $3.99 a yard. One yard of fabric can yield many conjuring bags, several spirit dolls, an altar cloth, quite a few petition squares and more, giving you the opportunity to complete many projects for pennies on your hard-earned dollar!

The amount of time taken to grunge the material adds to the power of the poppet. These dolls have a different aura—one that I believe carries more power, particularly if you have painted the doll or animal.

Standard Grunge Liquid Bases

Coffee: Either coffee brewed dark and allowed to cool or instant coffee. Coffee is often associated with the planet Mars because it is a stimulant, although I've also seen a rulership book that puts the brew under Neptune. To me, coffee isn't wishy-washy, so I stick with the Mars correspondence. Here, coffee would stand for movement, starting things, heating situations up, etc. A bit of honey or brown sugar can be added to the coffee during the brewing process for an extra kick in attraction magick.

Tea: Brewed dark and allowed to cool. Tea is ruled by the sun and is thought to promote good fortune, great riches, courage, longevity, and strength.

Standard Grunge Ingredients

Cinnamon: Powdered works best for grunging. Cinnamon is ruled by the sun, so it speaks of success, healing, protection, and, of course, love.

Nutmeg: Powdered. Nutmeg falls under the expertise of Jupiter and is considered a "good luck" ingredient. Also associated with positive spirituality.

Vanilla: Liquid extract. Ruled by Venus. Vanilla has a variety of correspondences, including mental agility, love, lust, friendship, fast luck, and fast cash.

Allspice: Powdered. Another grunge ingredient that falls under the power of Mars. Allspice is associated with good fortune and luck as well as money magnet properties.

Orange Peel: Fresh. Steep the orange peel in the coffee liquid overnight and then remove. Ruled by the sun, orange correspondences include psychism, good luck, money drawing, passion, love, and cleansing.

Cloves: Powdered. Ruled by Jupiter and often used for protection, multiplying money, and love. A commanding herb. Cloves are also favored for banishing and cleansing.

Can you steep other herbs in your brewed coffee or tea? Absolutely! I normally choose food-safe herbals because of possible skin absorption when handling the finished product. For example, I wouldn't steep the cloth in wormwood as this can be toxic. However, if you were having trouble sleeping at night and you asked me to make you a conjuring bag, I would definitely steep lavender in the coffee mixture. Use your nose and your needs to make your choices.

Grunge Technique #1: General Supplies

- 2 clear bowls, large enough to hold about 4 cups of liquid—one to steep herbs and one to strain your finished brew

- 2 cups blessed water brewed into strong coffee or tea

- your chosen material, cut to size of project (conjuring bag, spirit doll, altar cloth, etc.)

- strainer (optional)

- spices of choice: I use one tablespoon of vanilla extract and 1 teaspoon of the other powdered ingredients already mentioned; however, you can choose the amount and type of herbs you desire

- wooden spoon (to stir the brew)

- sandpaper (optional)

- oven, hot sun, embossing dryer, or blow dryer (be careful with the last two—you can burn your material or yourself!)

- cookie sheet covered in tinfoil (so clean-up isn't messy)

General Magickal Set-Up Instructions

Know your purpose before you start, as the need orchestrates the timing, charms, and chants you may use, as well as deity choice. When you have the need set in your mind, cleanse and consecrate all equipment and supplies. Morning energy is great for general projects of this nature, although if I were going to make you a conjuring bag for protection, I might choose midnight, and, if I could, wait for a Scorpio moon. If I wanted to make a conjuring bag for money or business profit, then I would choose noon under a Leo or Taurus moon. Finally, if I wanted to make a healing bag, I might wait for a Cancer moon, particularly if I wanted to make such a bag for a close friend or family member.

Instructions for Staining Unpainted Fabric

Step 1: Brew coffee or use instant coffee and hot water. If using tea, make a strong brew.

Step 2: Add spices and herbals. Allow mixture to cool.

Step 3: Strain spices and herbs out of brew. Some folks just leave all the coffee grounds and spices in the bowl, grinding the cloth into the mixture and brushing the cloth off after baking.

Step 4: Dip cloth into brew. You can remove immediately for a light stain or allow cloth to remain in the mixture for a deeper stain. Dip cloth repeatedly to make sure all areas are covered. Chant while you work!

Step 5: Remove cloth from brew and squeeze out excess liquid. At this point, some practitioners like to rub additional dry ingredients into the wet cloth, leaving them there through the baking process.

Step 6: Place flat on a cookie sheet and put into an 180-degree oven for 25 minutes. Check periodically to ensure cloth doesn't burn. You can also turn cloth over ten minutes into the baking time.

Step 7: Remove from oven; allow to cool. Brush off any herbals with a stiff brush or a bit of fine sandpaper. That's all there is to it!

Grunge Technique #2: Instructions for Staining Painted Fabric

This technique, as I stated earlier, is a little more involved and creates a stiffer finished piece. This type of grunging is often done after the project is completed, as the stiffer fabric is more difficult to sew and near impossible to stitch if you are doing something small, like a three-inch star, a doll, or small conjuring packet. The grunge technique #2 is the type used for all those nifty-neaty prim stuffed items (dolls, crows, cows, chickens, pillows) you see in the country specialty stores.

SUPPLIES

You will need the same supplies as in the first technique, along with the following:

• acrylic paint of your choice—use any color but know beforehand that the process dulls the color

• fine sandpaper

• a paper towel or two

• paint brush

INSTRUCTIONS

Step 1: With your chosen acrylic color, paint the project. For plain primitive work, burnt sienna is often chosen. Allow to dry.

Step 2: Lightly sand the surface of your project. There is no right way to do this. You can sand as hard or as light as you desire. The idea is to have a mottled appearance, so wrinkles in the fabric are just fine.

Step 3: Dip the project in the coffee spice brew from grunge technique #1. Rub extra spices all over the doll.

Step 4: In the 180-degree oven, bake the project for 25 minutes. Do not allow your project to burn. Flip it over halfway through.

Step 5: After cooling, brush off herbs. You can sand again—or not; your choice. When finished, use a paper towel to remove any powdered paint.

As I mentioned earlier, this technique creates a stiffer material. To loosen up the fabric, roll in your hands, bunch it, squeeze it, and roll again. This is a great time to add a specific chant or charm to infuse the fabric with focused energy.

From this point, you can turn your fabric into a compendium of enchanted items. When your project is finished, complete the magick with a spell or ritual that matches your intent.

You can use this technique to make squares of material into single petitions or turn them into enchanted packets filled with herbs, resins, and charms. You can also use them in scrapbooking. My only advice is to grunge a completed project, particularly if you wish to paint a doll. Trying to sew painted, grunged, sanded material is a nightmare you don't want to experience! Why do I grunge many of my more ornate dolls? I like the power the technique brings to the doll itself, and I like the idea that I am practicing a unique art. Not many individuals like to take the time required to grunge a doll, and therefore they are somewhat rare.

I like that. To me, it makes the doll all the more special and unusual—which is a glittering energy in itself.

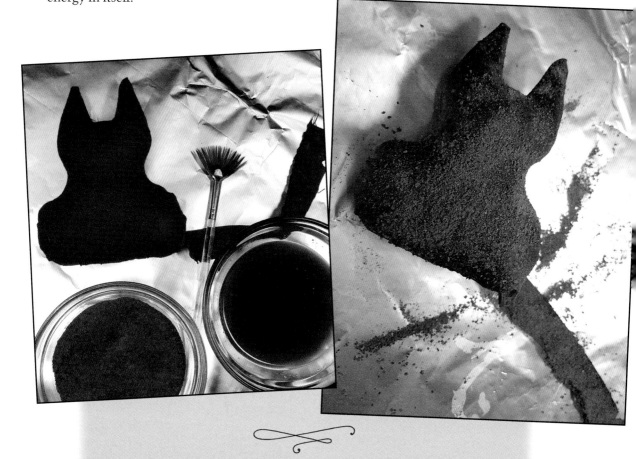

AFTER BAKING YOUR PROJECT, ALLOW TO COOL COMPLETELY,
THEN BRUSH OFF EXCESS GRUNGING MIXTURE

I USED GRUNGED MATERIAL FOR TACO CAT, THE SHEEP,
AND THE MYSTICAL HALLOWEEN DOLL IN THIS PHOTO

The Choice of Clay or Wax

There are many types of clay on the market today, some that air dry and others that require baking in your kitchen oven or firing in a kiln. There are clays that can be painted and those where paint does not adhere well. Some clays harden quickly and others never dry. Each type of clay manipulates differently in the hands. Although you can create cavities in clay poppets to add herbs and charms, unless your poppet is huge, usually only a small amount (which is enough) can be inserted and still maintain the shape of the body.

In magick it is thought that if the clay hardens well, then the image can protect or harden (as in hardening someone's heart). If the clay is malleable or your material is beeswax, then the image can be coerced, particularly if the figure is prepared when the moon is in the sign of Pisces or when aspects to Neptune are pleasant. Try different types of clay to see which works best for you. Easily manipulated clay or wax also can be used to change sickness into health. Poppets also can be constructed out of beeswax sheets using cookie cutters.

Tools for Clay, Wax, or Soap

Constructing items with decorative clay is a hot hobby these days that has generated many wonderful tools to ease the work. Some practitioners prefer to only use their fingers when molding poppets, while others enjoy the use of acrylic brayers, cookie cutters, wooden or metal smoothing tools, molds, and more.

A HAND-OPERATED PASTA MACHINE IS AN EXCELLENT
INVESTMENT IF YOU PLAN TO WORK OFTEN WITH CLAY

When working with polymer clays such as Premo or Sculpey, a pasta machine is often used to help make the clay quickly malleable. If you plan on using polymer clays to design jewelry or amulets in addition to poppets, you may wish to invest in a pasta machine. Not only does it save your hands, but you can also mix colors and create truly eye-popping color blends in a variety of thicknesses.

The formulas at the end of this book lend themselves well to the construction of amulets and talismans as well as poppets.

Wax can also be manipulated with clay tools (depending upon the type used). If you don't have access to clay or wax, you can even use a bar of soap or formulate your own base and pour into a mold, which allows you to easily add other items to the soap. I once poured a nine-banishing-herb-laced soap base into a human figure mold, allowed it to harden, and then placed the figure under constant running water to remove that individual's negativity from my life. It worked extremely well.

Should you wish to carve your soap poppet, the harder soaps are a little more difficult to cut; the softer soaps, however, may crumble. You may want to take a trial run with the tools you've chosen and different brands of soap until you find one that suits your handling style best.

What Is the Life Expectancy of Your Poppet?

When choosing the fabric and other items, consider the life expectancy of your poppet. Is this an issue where you will want to burn the poppet immediately or is the poppet for attracting a more long-term state, such as good fortune for the family? If you want to burn the poppet, make sure you don't pick flame-retardant materials. If you want the poppet to disintegrate over time—for example, burying it off your property—you may want fabric that will rot quickly (such as a thin muslin). Do you want to make a poppet for your daughter to receive a promotion? When she gets that promotion, how will you dispose of the poppet? If you made the poppet in the image of your daughter, you don't want to burn it or harm it in any way. Instead, you will want to decommission the poppet (dissolve the magick and take apart the poppet) in ceremony. You will find instructions for decommissioning/deactivating a poppet later in this book.

How to Handle an Unfinished Poppet
Cloth, paper, or other medium

There may be times when you have started to make a poppet and then changed your mind about the intent or the proposed use of the doll, or circumstances suddenly change, making the completion of the poppet unnecessary. Too, there is the possibility of crossed conditions—although this is rare, it does happen—when everything seems to go wrong with the construction of the doll, and you feel angry or frustrated with it. Don't keep going for the sake of completion. Stop.

With all three examples, sprinkle what you have done with holy water, take it apart, and either burn or throw away the doll. If you are feeling angry, realize that something is not right either with the wording of your intent or the doll's main purpose. Sometimes Spirit steps in when we are blindly forging ahead; acknowledge this power and let the doll go. Wait twenty-four hours, consider your intent again, reword it, and try to build another doll from brand-new materials. If the crossed condition still exists, do a personal cleansing ritual. Then, if you feel the doll is still necessary, once again rework your intent and proceed.

The more magick you do on a daily basis, the stronger you become. There will be times when conditions are so right that your desire manifests before the doll is completed. You can either finish the doll and then ritually deactivate it, thanking Spirit for the speedy answer to your request, or you can simply deactivate the unfinished doll, thanking Spirit for the quick fulfillment. This may occur for you repeatedly when the moon is in a particular sign. This is your cue that the moon in that sign is a very good time for you. A Sagittarius moon can also render a quick completion.

Secrecy

Although you may have read otherwise, secrecy is of the utmost importance when creating, birthing, and empowering a poppet. I always advise my students not to tell anyone what they are doing because the moment you plug someone else into that network, they also become bonded with the project (even if they don't mean to be). Their opinions and personal energy can harm the work, stall it, or completely disarm all the effort expended. To be silent brings great rewards.

Stuffing for Cloth Poppets

You can use a variety of mediums for stuffing your poppet. From top left, the picture above shows traditional white polyester fiberfill stuffing, oakmoss, Spanish moss, and plastic pellets. Buckwheat hulls are a favorite for dream pillows as well as dolls. Mugwort herb can also be used. Try combining different types of stuffing in one poppet. For example, stuff the head and arms with fiberfill and the remaining body with a combination of specially selected herbs for spellcasting that matches the intent of the poppet. Finish off with a bit of oakmoss, mugwort, or perhaps some lavender.

If you would like your poppet to have bendable arms and legs, cut pipe cleaners and lay them onto the poppet before stitching it. Tack in place with Liquid Stitch, Tacky Glue, or E600 glue. While pipe cleaners can be inserted when you are almost done sewing and before stuffing, they can sometimes be difficult to wiggle into the poppet, so

PLACE AND TACK PIPE CLEANERS IN PLACE
BEFORE SEWING IF YOU WANT THE LIMBS TO BEND

tacking them in before sewing lowers the frustration. Many practitioners choose to work directly on their altar or on a candleboard like the one shown in the picture. This runic board made of wood is a perfect surface, as you can create and then cast the spell all on the same empowered area.

Basic Ritual Items You May Need

Every practitioner has his or her own way of performing magick. Some magickal workers like a ceremonial format, others a more practical folk approach, and there are several who like to mix ceremonial and folk together, creating a surprisingly smooth blend of manifestation. Regardless of which type of ritual activity you choose, what is important is the result. The question that should always be asked is: Did it work?

Over the years you will develop your own style of working magick. Your practices become an amalgam of your thoughts, experiences, training, beliefs, and techniques. No two magickal practitioners ever work exactly the same way.

The ritual items and practices suggested here are just that—suggestions. They are what I often use as a part of my magickal working when creating and energizing a poppet. I don't always use all the supplies listed; rather, I try to match my intent, my feelings, and the purpose of the working into a fluid, enchanting experience. You should always feel good about what you are doing. If you carry any doubt, this will hamper your overall success.

General Ritual Supply List

SALT: Salt is a marvelous spiritual cleanser. Before poppet construction, all items can be buried in salt for at least twenty-four hours to remove negativity. Salt can also be used to make holy water, another item that can be generously used throughout the poppet creation process. If the doll in process is subjected to any negativity while you are working, bury it in salt for at least twenty-four hours before continuing.

WATER: Water takes on whatever thoughts are given. If you bless it, the water flows that positive energy into anything. If you curse it, the water carries the charge of aggression or stagnation. Blessed water (aka holy water) can be used to begin any poppet project. Cursed water or stagnant water can be used in defense to bring karma to bear or cause chaos among the evil, but only after the doll has been completed. I always place a fresh glass of clear blessed water on the table when I am designing, sewing, or decorating any poppet. Some practitioners believe that when water bubbles in a glass, it is a signal that Spirit is pleased with the working.

INCENSE OR SMUDGE STICK: The smoke carries thoughts and prayers to Spirit and can also be used to fumigate a poppet, imbuing the material with a particular psychic pattern. For example, when making a guardian angel poppet, passing the materials several times over a censor of frankincense or a stick of burning Nag Champa incense ensures that the higher vibrations intended stay with the materials during the creation process. The same can be said for holy water. Not all poppets only take an hour or so to create. Sometimes you may work on a poppet for several days before you feel you've gotten it just right. In that time span a great deal can occur in your life, and many people can enter or leave the working area. Daily life doesn't cease simply because you are making a poppet. Perhaps there is dinner to cook, a sporting event to attend, work to do around the house, a job to hurry to…life swirls around your poppet. Using incense, a sage stick, sweetgrass, or holy water frequently throughout the construction process helps to keep the working clean of unwanted energies, including your own thoughts that may not match your original intent. Incense can also help to set your intent. For example, if you wanted to make a poppet for action, you may choose to burn cinnamon or dragon's blood incense while stitching the material together. Perfume can take the place of incense if you don't like the smoke; if you are going only for aroma, try using soy wax melts or tarts in an electric burner, which can heighten the working through the vibrations of scent.

FIRE: Use candles or a cauldron, depending upon your proposed activities. Fire is used to bless and to instill energy into the working. Ideally, any candles used should match the intent of the poppet, either in color, scent, or both. If you are making a doll for action, then burn a red, cinnamon-scented candle while working. If you don't like the smoke from paraffin candles, try using soy candles with cotton wicks, which cut the smoke by about 98 percent. If you don't have a wide selection of colors, white will always work. I often roll my own beeswax candles, adding specific powders, oils, and liquid fluid condensers to match a particular working. For example, I love to use purple, violet-scented candles that I make myself, employing astrological timing as my guide on when to pour the wax so that the candle can lend as much power to my working as possible. If the problem the doll is addressing is particularly difficult, I will roll several candles of different colors and burn the heavier colors first, followed by the lighter ones. Because I am an artist, I see shadows first and move toward the light; I understand that there is no real color, only light, only hue.

YOU CAN MAKE YOUR OWN BLESSED CANDLE CONTAINERS TO
MATCH ANY WORKING. SHOWN HERE IS A PAINTED JELLY JAR
WITH A PENTACLE PRINTED ON MUSLIN AND GLUED TO THE FRONT.
THE ENTIRE OUTSIDE IS THEN SEALED WITH ACRYLIC SEALER.

USING YOUR OWN MAGICKAL OILS AND FLUID
CONDENSERS CAN RAMP UP THE POWER OF ANY DOLL.
ORANGE CHILI PEPPER IS ONE OF MY FAVORITES TO
USE FOR SUCCESS AND MOTIVATION DOLLS.

MAGICKAL OIL OR LIQUID FLUID CONDENSERS: Scented oil consisting of a carrier combined with essential oils or fragrances is used to link the physical, mental, and spiritual applications of your intent. Oils are employed to "dress" or "bless" people and objects, raising the vibration of the person or object and linking those vibrations to the desire. You can make your own oil formulas or purchase them. Perfume can be used in place of a magickal oil. I use the oils that I make myself to dress ritual candles and the petitions or paper sigils that I place inside the doll. I make my own oils so that I can harvest certain herbs and flowers at the height of their season with the most applicable magickal timing. I also used liquid fluid condensers in the preparation and enchantment of most of my dolls. For complete instructions on how to make your own liquid fluid condenser, please refer to my book *The Witching Hour*. The use of a liquid fluid condenser ramps up the power of your working exponentially.

RITUAL SURFACE OR ALTAR: I make most of my poppets on a special candleboard that I constructed for my Braucherei (Pow-Wow) and whisper magick work. A candleboard is a portable altar usually made of natural materials such as wood, stone, clay, or metal. I use wood, stone, and copper frequently. Other practitioners choose an inspiring altar cloth or other magickally decorated surface. Sometimes I place my entire sewing machine right on my table altar. I know a woman who makes all her poppets on the island in her kitchen because the island happens to sit not only in the center of the kitchen but in the center of the house as well, drawing on the power of the placement.

A POPPET TRUNK AND BOX (LEFT)

AND A SPECIAL BAG (RIGHT) FOR STORAGE

Poppet Boxes or Trunks: I use ritually cleansed boxes and trunks to house my supplies while working on a particular poppet. This way, if I am working on the construction of a poppet, I can put the materials away during family time or when I'm interrupted by an event, phone call, or other family duty. The box or trunk also serves as a collection area as I work on the poppet; for example, I may have chosen the charms and herbs for inclusion but haven't sewn the poppet yet (as in the picture). Since I sometimes work on more than one poppet at a time, or while working on one poppet a need arises to create a different one, I have more than one ritually cleansed storage box. The poppet shown in the picture is for mental clarity on a love issue. The crystal in the picture is cleansed every time I put a different poppet in the box. The trunk in the picture was purchased. I made the box from a cigar box using paper, black paint, and an acrylic sealer. I have also provided instructions for the reversal box later in this book.

Birthing Pot or Box: As a part of the empowerment process, all of my poppets and dolls are wrapped in a triple layer of unbleached muslin and placed for three days in a Braucherei birthing pot or box. The layers of cloth around the poppet keep it from getting dirty. The birthing pot is a glass or clay container filled with dirt and a small blend of herbs that correspond with my purpose. At dawn at the beginning of the fourth day, the doll is removed from the pot and placed in black cloth to protect it from harmful energies. The black cloth is removed when you are ready to command the doll, which can be done that day or a day when the astrological correspondences are auspicious for the poppet's purpose. A birthing pot can be of any style or size—ceramic, clay, or wood is best. I do not recommend using plastic. I have a large black birthing box with lid painted with a psychic eye that is used for my larger dolls. This box is lined with black felt (see next page for photo).

Special Bag: I use various techniques to keep project pieces together to protect them from being influenced by random acts. For some, I keep in-progress pieces in a special bag I made with a magickal sigil printed on a section of cloth that I stitched onto the bag. For larger dolls, I have wooden boxes to store the doll and its associated objects while in the creation process. Cloth, jewelry, hair, items collected on spirit walks, etc., go into the box. This helps me keep theme items with the right project. Depending upon the future owner, I may add other things to the boxes or bags such as the owner's name, photograph, astrological information, likes, needs, etc. To help the doll come into its birthing process, I also add activation herb packets and gemstones that are associated with the owner's needs. In my mind, the longer all the items are together in the box, the better the "take" when the ritual blending and activation process begins. The most important mindset in the creation of your magickal vehicle, whether it be a doll, an animal, or an amusing mythical shape, is to carry no judgement—meaning don't let the mind wander into fear-based "what-ifs." Work in peace; there is more power there.

I DESIGNED THIS BIRTHING BOX WITH A PSYCHIC EYE
ON THE LID FOR MY LARGER SPIRIT DOLLS (TOP)

YOU MAY WISH TO DESIGN, CLEANSE, AND EMPOWER
A BIRTHING BOX OR JAR (BOTTOM)

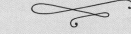

A SUCCESS POPPET AND ITS INGREDIENTS

Choosing Spell Ingredients for Your Poppet

All items that you place in your poppet should match your intention. The number and type of ingredients are entirely up to you and depend upon your intent, what you have available, and the medium of your poppet (cloth, clay, vegetable, etc.). For example, ingredients are often stuffed in a cloth poppet but are "dressed" on a stick or clay poppet because including large objects within the clay or in the sticks isn't really an option (unless you make a very large clay doll or hollow out the sticks you are using). For clay or sticks, spell ingredients can be turned into embellishments on the outside of the poppet (dressing) or placed in a conjuring bag that will accompany the poppet. Small clay poppets can be used as an ingredient in a magical pouch, gris-gris bag, or sachet. The success poppet pictured above includes mint, sunflower petals, mari-gold petals, Low John, a buckeye, elecampane, a golden success trinket, and a petition dressed with cedar oil. Let me make it perfectly clear that a formula or idea in this book is just that—a formula or idea. The true magick, power, and force emanates from within yourself. Don't get hung up on ingredient choices or amounts as in the idea of right or wrong. You aren't baking a cake that could be ruined if you miss an ingredient. There is no accurate measurement for combining the spiritual and the material. Above all, your dolls should be the manifestation of your joy in the completion of your task. Do not lose sight of the visionary whole in the tedium of correctness.

Ingredients can include:

- herbs and roots—single additives or magickal powders (Although I have many formulas in this book, for additional information you may enjoy my book *The Witching Hour*, which is dedicated to magickal powders and herbal sachets.)

- paper petitions or sigils (I have provided several in this book; however, there is no end to what words, symbols, or sigils you can put in a poppet or spirit doll. Pseudo-Paracelsus in *Liber Secundus Archioxis Magicae* in 1570 states: "Characters, words and seals themselves possess a secret strength that is no wise contrary to nature and has no link whatsoever with superstition! Furthermore, it should not appear extraordinarily impossible to you that medicine can offer relief to man not by means of absorption but by being worn around the neck in the manner and custom of a seal" (Lecouteux 2002, 31). It was believed that the essence of the word could "sink and link" particular energies to any person, place, or thing. What you write or draw these sigils on is also important in your work. Brown paper for earth magick and prosperity. Real paper money is also used as a foundation for prosperity sigil work. Naturally shed snakeskin works very well for the protection of self, animals, and family or loved ones. Paper you make yourself with a press from selected herbs can be extremely powerful, particularly for healing magick.)

- an item that represents the person or energy, or an item from an individual, such as hair or fingernail clippings; often called mummiel magick (Bardon 1956, 200) or a taglock

- magnets or dressed lodestones (lodestones dotted with an attraction oil, universal fluid condenser, or attraction fluid condenser)

- photographs (You can put the photograph right in the doll, glue the photo on the face of the doll, or make a copy of the photograph. There is also a printable fabric where you can print your entire photograph on fabric, then cut out what you need. For the home poppet maker, I would suggest using an Epson brand printer as the ink doesn't fade or wash out like its competitors. Printing directly on the material gives you an incredibly unique-looking doll.)

- hard candy, sugar, or beeswax (For drawing the sweetness of life, money, and joy to the working. Hard candy is often used because it disintegrates slower. For example, a doll made to help you in holiday shopping might contain a magnet to get the deals, three hard peppermint candies, and a lock of your own hair. This doll can last for several years without worrying about the candy rotting. As a note, candy is often used to entice good spirits to help you in your work.)

- grave dirt (Where in the cemetery and from whose grave is important.)

- dirt from a profitable business such as a bank, department store, or an establishment that relates to your request (Research the profitability and strength of the place. For example, not all banks are strong, and some businesses may be ready to go under—you don't want negative energy in your own success working. It is worth it to check the stock market, pay attention to the business section of the newspaper, etc.)

- dirt or scrapings from a foot track (where a person has stepped) or where they have been seated for any length of time (Sybil Leek tells us in her book *Cast Your Own Spell* that "it is a widespread belief in Germany that if a piece of grass turf holds a man's footprint, it can be taken up and dried and used for magickal purposes" [Leek 1970, 149].)

- resins such as frankincense, copal, and myrrh

- burned paper or ashes

- money (bills or coins) (This should never be stolen or obtained from negative sources, such as a drug deal. Cleanse all money before use.)

- crystals or gems

- religious items

- animal claws, teeth, feathers, or fur (Often used in spirit animal dolls to strengthen the connection of the doll to the represented animal. Note that these items are not harvested in pain, they are often found in the wild or are clippings or trimmings from domesticated animals. Shed snakeskin is extremely useful in the banishment of evil.)

- an individual's phone number (These days most people carry their cell phones all the time; use the magick of their phone number to connect them to the doll.)

- keys (To symbolically open locks—extremely useful for dolls associated with overcoming blocks or breaking through to a new level of understanding.)

- the Himmelsbrief or Prayer of Protection (See opposite page—this is usually anointed with holy water and wrapped around a lock of hair, then wrapped with red thread. Spit on the thread to hold the power. For example, if the doll is for your child, the Himmelsbrief is wrapped around a lock of your hair because you are the genetic link and designated protector of your child. A wife would put in her hair for her husband, or a husband would put in his hair for his wife. This is a Pennsylvania German practice.)

- matches (Used to represent the fire of life. I always light a match and drop the lit match into the body of a spirit doll, then quickly extinguish the flame with the doll itself. This is a little dangerous, but it is one way I breathe life into the doll—I fan the flame once with my breath, then extinguish it. In my mind, this action pulls all the ingredients together, which I quickly visualize, and then empowers them with the life of my cause.)

THIS BINDING POPPET
CONTAINS CLOVE, WILLOW
BARK, LOBELIA, SLIPPERY
ELM, A PETITION DRESSED
WITH BINDING MAGICKAL
OIL, AND DIRT FROM THE
GATES OF A GRAVEYARD

*Letter of Protection
for*

_____

In the names of the Lord and Lady,

Whoever beareth this letter upon the self shall
not dread the enemy, nor be overcome, nor
suffer injury nor misfortune, nor fear flood, fire,
weapons, chemicals, poison, gossip, ill will, bullies,
thieves, murderers, rapists, liars, nor be affected
in any way by self same, nor be captured, face
torture, nor fear weather nor war, nor suffer in
any way, nor suffer mental anguish of any kind.

Whoever beareth this letter will be filled with
strength, mental acuity, protection, and love.

They shall sense unseen dangers and
respond accordingly. They shall overcome
and persevere where others fall.

They shall return home victorious
and live a full and active life.

In the name of the Perfection of the Universe,

So Mote It Be!

THE HIMMELSBRIEF, OR PRAYER/LETTER OF PROTECTION

The number of items chosen is often picked in sets of three, seven, or nine; however, use your intuition to decide how many items to include. If it feels good and there is no hesitation, you know you are on the right track.

Magickal oils or liquid fluid condensers are often used to dress sigils and petitions that are included in the body of a stuffed cloth doll. To "dress" is to rub the oil or condenser on the paper clockwise or counterclockwise, depending upon the intent of the petition. Some practitioners draw an equal-armed cross, pentacle, or other design on the paper with the oil. The photo below shows a triangular-shaped petition dressed with Jupiter Oil.

If you are using clay, a few drops of magickal oil, liquid fluid condenser, magickal powder, or all three can be massaged directly into the polymer clay before the formulation of the doll. The photo on the opposite page shows a protection oil and finely ground magickal protection powder that will be added to the clay ball. A hole can be created in the belly of a clay poppet to hold a special blend of magickal powder, as in the photo. Before completion, the cavity will be covered with clay. The hands and legs are stuck together to symbolically "stick" the representation with his own negativity and keep him

THIS TRIANGULAR PROTECTION SIGIL
IS DRESSED WITH JUPITER OIL

from doing further harm. This poppet was taken to an ancestor's grave with a petition that the person it represented be removed from his place of employment, where he was systematically harming his coworkers, and that he be blessed with healing energy and an opportunity for rehabilitation. I also positioned a rolled beeswax chime candle over the hole and cast a spell as the candle burned down and dripped over the figure. The poppet worked quite well.

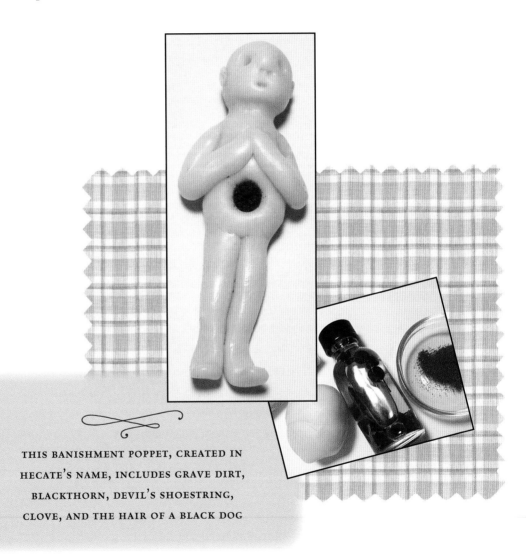

THIS BANISHMENT POPPET, CREATED IN
HECATE'S NAME, INCLUDES GRAVE DIRT,
BLACKTHORN, DEVIL'S SHOESTRING,
CLOVE, AND THE HAIR OF A BLACK DOG

General Cleansing for Supplies

This photo shows what my candleboard looks like when preparing for a general cleansing of my supplies. I already know my intent: a poppet to bring mental clarity on a love issue for a friend. I chose blue for clarity and harmony of thought, and the red heart to represent the love issue. This poppet will contain lavender (cleansing of the mind), rose petals (right navigation), and a bay leaf (protection and wishes) on which I will write my petition. The blessed water, salt, and candle will be used to cleanse and bless all items on the candle board, which include the needles I will use, the cut poppet, thread, magickal oil, herbs and bells for inclusion in the poppet, the eyes, and the beads that will be used for embellishment. The magickal oil chosen for this working is a Mercury Oil, which consists of jojoba carrier and herbs associated with the planet Mercury. The bells are a symbol of clarity. As a note, this combination could also be used for clarity on one's job, although I would add devil's shoestring (to clear the way and hobble enemies). When the weather is warm, I cleanse and bless my supplies outside and many times incorporate a sage stick into the working. In the winter I do not use the sage stick or incense during the general cleansing. The choice of what you use is entirely up to you. Missing in the example is the photograph of the person the poppet represents and the taglocks (hair, fingernails, a piece of clothing that belongs to the person) belonging to the individual.

General Cleansing Rite for Supplies

What prayers, chants, or charms you use during a cleansing rite are entirely up to you. These prayers or chants don't always have to be the same; you may prefer to gear your words and actions to the intent of the poppet or you may have a specific prayer or chant that you always use. When I was first learning magick, I followed strict rules, using the same format every time. As I grew older and learned more, I began to trust my intuition in my magickal choices. If I feel calm, directed, harmonious, or joyful, I know that I am following the right wording for the task at hand. If I do not feel good about what I am doing, I stop, rethink, and proceed only when I have reached that mental state of "right." I have even destroyed poppets halfway through completion if I don't feel like they will do the proper job. At first I vacillated, not wanting to be wasteful of materials or effort, but I have learned that if the poppet goes hinkey, the magick will not conclude in the way needed. Start over!

For performing a cleansing and blessing rite, I always face east and take at least three cleansing breaths before I begin, running the energy up from the ground and into my body to the top of my head as I inhale, then concentrating on running the energy into my hands as I exhale. Once I have done this at least three times, I speak my own words of power—sometimes formally, sometimes informally—that will connect me to Spirit, or that which runs the universe. For example:

> *There is one power, which is the God and the Goddess, which is perfect in truth,*
> *clarity, order, and mutual good. I conjure cleansing energy into these objects using*
> *the sacred vehicles of fire, salt, water, and breath.*

Next, I will pick up the candle, rub it in my hands, and call on the assistance of Spirit to fill the candle with cleansed and blessed energy. Sometimes I dress the candle with magickal oil or a liquid fluid condenser by dotting a bit on the candle and continue to rub it in my hands. When I feel confident, I blow on the candle at least three times, running that energy into the candle with my breath, and then say "Only the good remains." I then light the candle and draw three equal-armed crosses in the air over the candle to seal the intent of cleansing and blessing.

Salt follows fire. I stir the salt with my finger, asking that all negativity and evil be removed from the salt. I circle the salt three times with the candle flame, then blow on the salt three times, running the energy into the salt with my breath, ending with the statement "Only the good remains." I draw three equal-armed crosses in the air over the salt to seal the intent of cleansing and blessing.

Water follows salt in the same manner. I ask Spirit to cleanse the water of all evil or negativity, ask for blessings, circle the water three times with the candle flame, add three pinches of salt, and run the energy with my breath as I blow at least three times on the water, ending with the statement "Only the good remains." I draw three equal-armed crosses in the air over the water to seal the intent of cleansing and blessing.

Now it is time to cleanse and consecrate everything on the candleboard. Again, you can use a chant, charm, or prayer as you cleanse and bless everything with the fire, salt, water, and your breath. You can also add your intent during the initial cleansing and blessing process. For example, I might pick up the poppet, cleanse it with fire, cleanse it with salt, cleanse it with water, and then say something like this:

> *I conjure thee, O poppet, that you will be for (person's name) a vehicle for clarity of thought. May you be cleansed and blessed, your purpose to that end.*

Or I might pick up the bells, cleanse them with fire, cleanse them with salt, cleanse them with water, and say:

> *I conjure thee, O bells, so that you will be for (person's name) a vehicle for clarity of thought. Each time your sound is heard, peace of mind transcends. May you be cleansed and blessed, your purpose to that end.*

I finish by blowing on the bells three times, running the energy up from the ground into my crown chakra as I breathe in, then running the energy out into my hands and into the bells as I exhale.

Remember to draw an equal-armed cross over every item you cleanse and bless to seal your work.

The Blending Process

Once you have cleansed and blessed each item, it is time to marry those energies together and close the rite. To finish, I often hold my hands over all the items, moving my hands in a particular circular direction that feels comfortable, breathing in deeply, moving the energy up from the ground and into my crown chakra as I inhale and then moving the energy down and into my hands as I exhale and out onto the items on the candleboard. I may end with something like this:

> I *conjure and command thee, O blend of sweet energy, that thy marriage be*
> *complete within this poppet and that by thy activation thou workest for the good of*
> *(person's name).*

Yes, I know my wording is a bit archaic; I think it is in the genes. You can certainly word your intent differently. I envision everything on the candleboard glowing with white or golden light and say (and this is the most important statement):

> I *know you will do this for me.*

I follow this statement with:

> As *above, so below, this working is sealed. Only the good remains.*

To seal the entire working, I draw an equal-armed cross in the air three times over the items on the candleboard.

Please note that this ceremony is not the empowerment nor the spellwork or "sending" of the completed poppet, it is just the beginning—the preparation for the strong magick to come!

This general rite is only a guideline for cleansing and blessing your supplies. Some of you may feel that it is too formal; others may think there isn't enough formality for your taste. Others may wish to exclude some elements or change them around, and that's fine. The only right way is the way that is comfortable for you—the way that brings the knowing that the magick will work.

three

Basic Poppet Construction
Stitching, Stuffing, and Spellcraft

Everything is connected. All of it. Every sound, every image, every person, each energy, all plants, animals, minerals, and elements—all are connected. All are part of the sea of potential that you can access at any time. You need only acknowledge that the connection exists and that you have the ability to access anything you desire. When you make a poppet, you are stitching, blending, and building a new connection to the fabric of the universe and to a desire in particular.

Making a Felt Poppet

Copy the poppet pattern of your choice on plain paper. You can also trace your pattern on freezer paper, then lightly iron the waxed side of the paper directly on the felt. After the paper cools, cut the shape out of both paper and felt. This saves a lot of snipping headache. When working with felt, the sharper the scissors, the better!

Cut out the pattern, pin it to two pieces of fabric, and cut the fabric around the pattern. You do not have to leave a seam allowance as most poppets are stitched with wrong sides together, leaving raw edges. Felt is often a preferred medium because it doesn't fray. Remove the pattern and pin the two pieces of fabric together so that the sides match evenly. If they do not, trim before sewing.

Should you choose to glue your poppet together, my advice is to use a glue gun rather than bottled glue. I've tried a number of glues with felt and have been regularly dissatisfied. Tacky Glue will hold for a time, but if you are looking for the most stable choice for a long-lasting spirit animal or doll, the glue gun tops the list.

If you want to mix stitching and gluing (as I did with the chakra fish in chapter 5), avoid placing glue where you will be sewing, as poking a needle through the glue can be very difficult. If you can't avoid it, keep a larger sharp needle available to poke a hole in the material first, then sew (like the old-fashioned sewing cards).

For my felt creations, I use two kinds of embroidery thread: standard, wherein you have to split the skein into three threads through the needle, and cotton perle, which is so much easier to handle and you don't have to fuss with splitting the threads. The only drawback to using the perle lies in the needle choice, mainly if you are going to do beadwork as well. Because the perle thread is heavier, make sure you have several sizes of needles that can accommodate the weight.

WHEN WORKING WITH
FELT, THE SHARPER THE
SCISSORS, THE BETTER

Add Embellishments or Extra Appendages
Before Sewing the Poppet Together

To make the construction of your poppet a breeze, add as many of your chosen stitched embellishments as possible before actually sewing the poppet together. Objects such as buttons, eyes, brads, rivets, crystals, beads, and sequins are much easier to sew on the top piece of your poppet before you make the poppet sandwich. This also makes a neater image, enabling you to hide knots. Animal tails and ears can also be tacked or secured, depending upon the construction of the image. If you will be turning the animal right-side out to finish, tack ears and tails to the reverse side, pointing inward. When you turn the animal out, the appendage will be secured in the seam and look great!

In the orange success poppet example shown here, the beadwork and button were applied before sewing the front and back of the poppet together (the poppet sandwich). In the green good fortune poppet, the eyes (pumpkin seeds held to poppet with brads and reinforced with a bit of glue) and the center green clover were affixed onto the poppet before sewing both sides together. A bead drilling tool was used to slowly puncture a hole in the pumpkin seed to avoid splitting the seed.

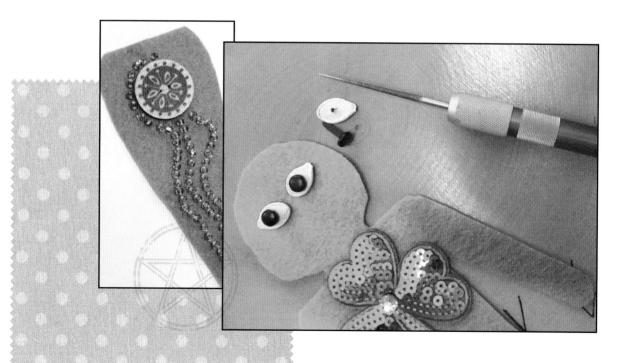

**IF THE EYES ARE FLAT, I OFTEN PLACE THEM
ON THE POPPET FACE BEFORE SEWING AND STUFFING;
JUST BE SURE TO KEEP THE EDGES OF THE EYES AWAY
FROM YOUR INTENDED SEAM ALLOWANCE**

**I SAVE ROSES THAT PEOPLE GIVE ME FOR SPECIAL OCCASIONS
AND DRY THEM TO USE IN POPPETS AND SPIRIT DOLLS**

To add a special kick to the above red love poppet, blessed rose petals dressed with Cleopatra love oil and rose liquid fluid condenser were inserted into the appliqué heart. A small lodestone or magnet could also be inserted into the pink heart before it is completely sewn shut. The button eyes were stitched onto the doll *before* sewing the front and back together. This really takes the hassle out of placing the eyes later!

Yarn can be used as hair or to give your poppet a unique look. Simply lay out the number of loops you desire on a flat surface, keeping them about the same size, then gather together. Pinch the loops together and lay the yarn on the back inside piece of the poppet. Tack into place with a bit of glue or use a few basting stitches. The final sewing of the poppet sandwich will keep the yarn firmly in place.

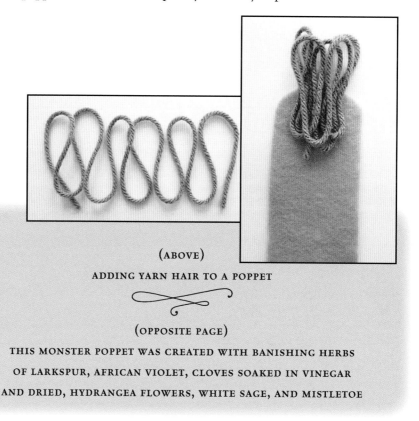

(ABOVE)

ADDING YARN HAIR TO A POPPET

(OPPOSITE PAGE)

THIS MONSTER POPPET WAS CREATED WITH BANISHING HERBS
OF LARKSPUR, AFRICAN VIOLET, CLOVES SOAKED IN VINEGAR
AND DRIED, HYDRANGEA FLOWERS, WHITE SAGE, AND MISTLETOE

You can take any shape and turn it into a unique spirit doll. Use different colors of felt to embellish your poppet, as in this monster-eater poppet. Cut three pieces of felt for your poppet sandwich instead of two. The third piece is a different color and can be trimmed to create fabric embellishments.

Cut the pieces of the different-colored felt into any shapes you desire. In this example, a sewing machine was used to quickly affix the pieces. Then, the front and back of the poppet were placed together and any excess purple trimmed away. The finished poppet is to ward off astral nasties, ghosties, nightmares, and things that go bump in the night. It is a perfect poppet for a child's room. If the young one is too small to play with the poppet (as the eyes and sequins are a choking hazard), hang the poppet near the top of a window.

Putting Your Poppet Together
"As I stitch thee, so I wish thee."

If you are planning to sew your poppet, you can either hand stitch or use a sewing machine. Choose which method (hand stitching or machine) suits your needs and your comfort level. Hand stitching can add more power and a greater connection with your intent to the materials. Chanting or singing activates the field of potential around the poppet. Your breath infuses the poppet with the life of the words.

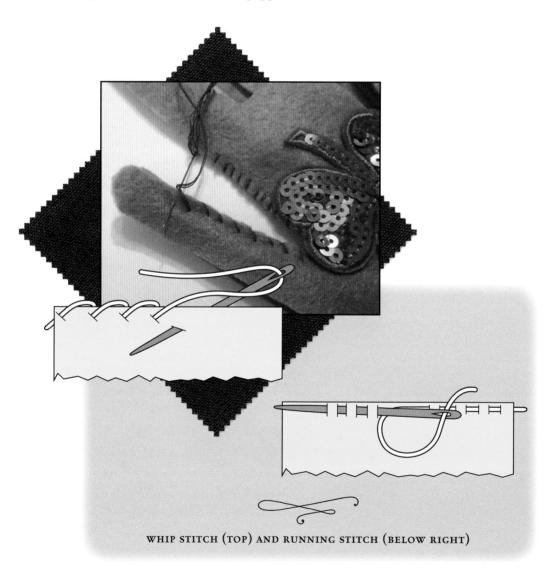

WHIP STITCH (TOP) AND RUNNING STITCH (BELOW RIGHT)

Chanting or singing as you stitch (whether it be hand work or machine) imbues the doll with a stronger link to your desire. Common hand stitches for closing poppets are the whip stitch and the blanket stitch. The running stitch can also be used.

You can also use fabric glue or a glue gun—just remember to leave an opening if you want to stuff your poppet and add special ingredients or a petition paper. Using a glue gun is a fast and simple way to put your poppet together. Be careful, however, if you plan to burn the poppet, as the glue could possibly create some harmful fumes.

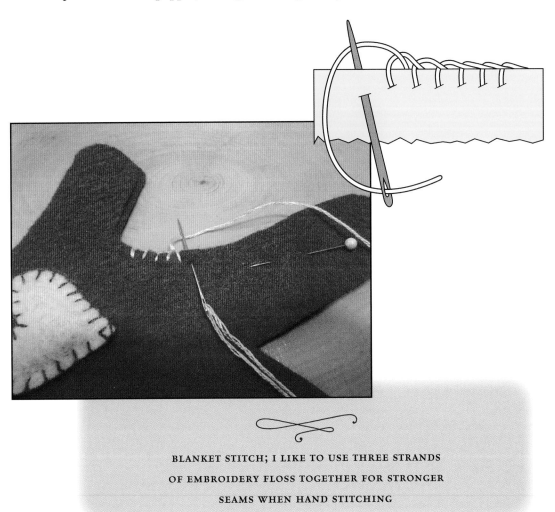

**BLANKET STITCH; I LIKE TO USE THREE STRANDS
OF EMBROIDERY FLOSS TOGETHER FOR STRONGER
SEAMS WHEN HAND STITCHING**

Stuffing As You Go

Before you begin sewing the poppet, consider where you will leave an opening for inserting the stuffing and additional ingredients. This decision is based on the shape of the poppet and the number and type of spell inclusions—you don't want to leave a small opening if you have a large buckeye to put inside. There is nothing more frustrating than quickly sewing a poppet together (for example, beginning on an arm or a leg) and then realizing that the opening you have left is insufficient for the ingredients you have, or even if you successfully stuff the poppet, your placement of the opening has made the hole difficult to close. To avoid these types of mistakes, I often stuff the image in stages, completing the head and the arms, then moving on to the trunk of the body.

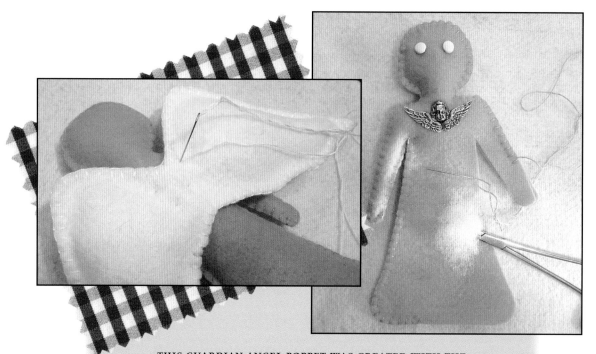

THIS GUARDIAN ANGEL POPPET WAS CREATED WITH THE
"STUFF AS YOU GO" TECHNIQUE, INSERTING STUFFING
INTO THE HEAD AND ONE ARM FIRST. WHEN I FINISHED
STITCHING THE SECOND ARM, I STUFFED THAT ARM
BEFORE STITCHING THE REMAINDER OF THE BODY.

WINGS WERE STITCHED AND STUFFED SEPARATELY, THEN TACKED
TO THE BACK OF THE BODY WITH A FEW QUICK STITCHES.

The "Come Alive" Technique

Many practitioners like to add specific cleansed and empowered items that match their intent, a photograph of the individual the doll represents, or a taglock into the body of the poppet right before they close the poppet. If you have already gathered, cleansed, and empowered these items, put them into the poppet now. This is the stage where I often insert a "come alive" petition—a piece of paper on which I have written a specific chant or charm that applies to the intent, as well as a "come alive" statement. The statement often differs, depending upon the intent. Any type of paper can be used for the "come alive" petition. The petition can be hand drawn (which is best) or computer printed, ornate or very simple. Sometimes I will use a simple "come alive" statement, and on other occasions the statement is extremely specific.

MY SHELF OF MAGICKAL HERBS AND
ITEMS THAT I USE IN MAKING SPIRIT DOLLS

A "COME ALIVE" PETITION WRITTEN ON BROWN PAPER

The "come alive" statement serves three purposes:

- It solidifies your intent.

- It ensures that any poppet you make can never be used against you. And if this is a very real worry for you (perhaps you make and sell your poppets), you can also add a specific statement that indicates the doll will lose all power should the owner try to use it against you or someone you love or use the doll in an unethical manner.

- It ensures that the poppet cannot be used in a way not intended.

If you are worried about someone opening the doll and reading what you have written, you can always use a magickal alphabet such as Theban, Angelic Script, or Passing the River. You can find these alphabets in many magickal books and on the internet. You may also like to try the method of "retrograde writing" used by the ancient Greeks when banishing or binding is required; this is writing your petition backwards. The ancient magicians often wrote chants, charms, names, and the intent on one side of the sigil and the name of a deity (the power you may be petitioning) on the opposite side of the paper.

My "come alive" petition almost always has the following inscription somewhere within the design:

> With breath of one, I come alive.
> With breath of two, I come alive.
> With breath of three, I am alive!

I then use this small incantation, with a slight change, when empowering or activating the doll. I either breathe into its mouth or into its heart chakra, repeating:

> With breath of one, you come alive.
> With breath of two, you come alive.
> With breath of three, (doll's name), you are alive!
> I command thee, (doll's name): live! Live! Live!
> And without my permission, thou shall never die!

Every practitioner eventually finds a set of magickal items, words, or designs that work extremely well for them. These things are not predicated on what someone tells you is right or what someone insists is the "right way." This amazing combination will be unique to you. For example, I have specific wording for most of my doll work. I always use kyphi oil to empower *all* my dolls. I *always* include the Egyptian ankh and the Egyptian Eye of Horus sigil. I always use my own personal magickal sigil-key that I developed myself for my work—sort of like a logo. I have a specific tuning fork to activate the dolls. Do not be afraid to use your own creativity and vibratory power.

Your magick is about your well-being and the good health of those you love. Magick is about being part of something greater than yourself, filled with compassion and love. That's the real magick.

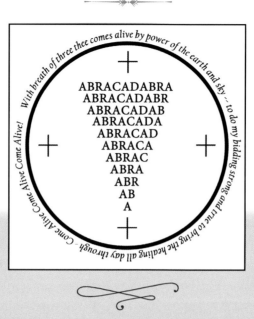

THIS ABRACADABRA SIGIL FOR BANISHING IS AN EXAMPLE
OF A COMPUTER-PRINTED CHARM TO BANISH ILLNESS WITH
A SPECIFIC ACTIVATION STATEMENT FOR THE POPPET

To many practitioners, just writing the chant or charm is not enough—it must be empowered so that the energy matches the words. The reasoning here is that you can say a string of words anytime and anywhere; however, if you wish to turn those words into magickal vehicles, where they have more strength and a better chance of manifestation, then empowerment is necessary for the creation and accurate direction of the force.

After I have prepared my "come alive" paper charm, I dress it with a magickal oil that matches my intent as well as a liquid fluid condenser. Then I intone various chants, depending upon the need. As I chant, I rub the paper in my hands, running the energy up from the ground and into my crown chakra as I inhale, and then into my hands and into the paper as I exhale. The empowerment depends upon the intent of the doll; the chant may echo the words I've written on the paper or it may be a general one, such as:

> From nothing to something, I will this doll to form—
> I know my intent will manifest and to this world be born.

I always chant any empowerment statement at least nine times, then I draw an equal-armed cross over the paper and fold it. If the doll is to draw something to the owner or me, I fold the paper toward myself. If the doll is to banish or repel a specific energy or problem, I fold the paper away from myself. I fold the petition as small as possible, making it easier to insert deeply into the body of the doll. The folded petition is often brushed with a liquid fluid condenser (that will match the type of magick that will be used in spellcasting) or with a universal liquid fluid condenser that can be used with any type of magickal operation.

THIS PETITION WAS DRESSED WITH VENUS OIL THAT I MADE DURING A TAURUS MOON ON A VENUS DAY IN A VENUS HOUR USING JOJOBA CARRIER AND VARIOUS HERBAL INGREDIENTS; THE PLANET VENUS IS KNOWN FOR ITS ATTRACTION ENERGY

THE PROSPERITY/MONEY POPPET (LEFT) CONTAINS REAL MONEY
(A BILL AND COINS), SASSAFRAS, A LODESTONE, GOLDEN
SAND, AND LODESTONE OIL I PREPARED MYSELF BY PLACING
LODESTONE CHIPS AND GOLDEN AND SILVER SAND IN A BOTTLE
OF MINERAL OIL FOR 30 DAYS (MOON TO MOON); I ALSO
ADDED 3 DROPS OF CORNUCOPIA LIQUID FLUID CONDENSER

THE LOVE POPPET (RIGHT) HAS A TINY PIECE OF LODESTONE
AND ROSE PETALS STUFFED UNDERNEATH THE HEART

Heart Packets

I often create "heart packets" (spell sachets)—small pouches that are red in color to manifest the energy heartbeat of the poppet. These packets contain a heart-shaped rose quartz pendant or stone, a sigil, herbs relating to the intent of the doll, a match, and three pennies (to pay the spirits).

Geist/Spirit Bag

The heart of the magickal doll or spirit animal is a conjure packet or sachet bag filled with herbs, charms, gemstones, prayers, natural objects, and/or a petition constructed in a ritualistic way and deposited deep inside the image. It is here where the intent of the doll links to specially selected items that will blend through sound, breath, and thought to create the doll's unique enchanted pattern. This "inside" power runs through the entire doll and jumps into action upon your command. I call this packet/sachet bag the geist bag, meaning spirit bag. It contains the essence of the doll in the world of spirit as well as the corporal world; the bag is a portal, a gate where energy moves from unmanifest to manifest upon your word. In some of my creations there is a second image—a secret one that nestles deep within the geist bag. This handcrafted creature is the "soul" of the doll or animal, known only to me.

One of the most valuable lessons about magick I've ever learned came from Llewellyn author Ray Malbrough. "Spellcasting," Ray would say, "is all about the process—from the idea to gathering the ingredients to creating a harmonious area in which to work, through the actual casting of the spell itself. Always remember," he said, "that the process, and where your head is at during that process, is the most important aspect. What you think during the entire progression will make or break your work."

Ray's way of teaching followed the Hermetic principles of vibration and rhythm. Everything has a heartbeat, a pattern, a rhythm of existence that ebbs and flows. Just as success has a rhythm and a vibration, so does poverty. Your thoughts determine which type of rhythm and vibration you tap in to and how far you ride with it. If you are continuously depressed, unhappy, and thinking angry thoughts, then you are attuning yourself to the negative. If you are upbeat and think, speak, and display ideas of success, then your entire vibrational pattern (and the area directly around you) will draw (attract) events, experiences, and people who also vibrate to positive ideas of success. Our emotions, as a result of our thoughts, create the pathway to either a successful vibration and rhythm or a pattern of failure. Where thought goes, energy flows.

With the principles of rhythm and vibration in mind, Ray's emphasis on celebrating the entire process of any working with enthusiasm is a sure way to reach any successful goal. In essence, you should enjoy all of it—the whole thing, the entire step-by-step process—to solidify the desired result. You wish to ride the pendulum to success, and, once that is reached, switch gears to the next successful cycle.

So, how do you do that? By being excited and happy about what you want to achieve, not worried or fearful or angry or irritated. Allow enthusiasm into the process. Key your emotions to that of joy, not sorrow. Invite creativity, happiness, and, yes, even laughter, into the activities surrounding your working(s). Be enthused about the objects you choose to enhance your work—the color, the texture, the sound, the aroma…all of it. Love every bit of it because what you love creates the emotional golden road to success.

Really.

It is that simple.

Why not take a moment and think about something happy—something that makes you smile. Tap out a rhythm on the table or desk beside your computer that mimics how you feel. This, then, is your primary rhythm of happiness. (If you don't like the New Age sound of the word "tap," then think "drum," as in drumming in a ritual circle.) You can use the sound pattern you choose for happiness when empowering your mojo/conjuring bags. Now, just for giggles, think of something you dislike; tap out a rhythm for that. Excellent! So! We want to avoid *that* type of emotional pattern while working on our conjuring bags, dollies, and spirit animals!

Consider each dolly or animal you make as a marvelous opportunity for a unique and fulfilling treasure hunt. Every item you place in that geist/spirit bag should mean something to you and make you excited that the object is going to be a part of the overall creation.

One way to empower your geist bag is through a color visualization that follows the chakras. Once you have blessed and cleansed all the things you wish to put in the bag, set them in an undisturbed place until you are able to perform your ritual or spellwork. When you are ready for the blending process, pick up each item and speak the intent of the doll (the purpose) aloud, letting your breath travel across the surface. One-word activation works best: for example, "healing," "joy," etc. I then drop a lit match in the bag to activate the contents with the light of Spirit. Tie the bag shut. I spray my geist bags with universal liquid fluid condenser as well as kyphi oil. Hold the bag between both palms at about the height of your heart chakra; some practitioners prefer the third-eye chakra. Close your physical eyes. Open your third eye. Connect your third eye to the throat chakra and then to the heart chakra. Take three deep breaths, blowing on the bag. Begin chanting (if you have a chant you would like to use) or repeating the one-word intention. In your mind begin visualizing the bag in your hands glowing, first with white light. Change the white light to purple, then to indigo (dark blue), then to light blue, to green, to yellow, to orange, and finally to red. Red, the root chakra, facilitates the manifestation of the desire on this plane of existence.

Declare: "So be it!" and draw an equal-armed cross over the bag when your concentration breaks to seal the working.

Put the geist/spirit bag in a safe place, covered with red cloth, until you place it in the doll or animal.

Can you change this ceremony? Certainly! Let your intuition be your guide.

Other Bags, Boxes, and Jars

You may also like to place your poppet in a special bag that has additional space for herbs, gemstones, or charms that you found after the doll's initial birthing ceremony. These bags can be of any shape, color, or style—the choice is entirely up to you. A few of your creations may "demand" a particular color bag, sachet pillow, or other charm. Gnomes and some small spirit animals seem to love glass jars where you can store new pennies, fun finds from the forest, unique gems, etc., along with the doll. I have an entire shelf of gnomes in jars—every jar is different, and every gnome has a unique skill. Some of my jars have solar light lids. I often set those jars on the porch rail outside during the day and bring them inside at night, where the soft light plays magickally across my altar.

MAGICKAL ITEMS DON'T ALWAYS HAVE TO BE PLACED IN
THE CENTER OF THE DOLL; IN THIS PHOTO, THE HERB
CINQUEFOIL (FIVE-FINGER GRASS) AND A HIMMELSBRIEF
WERE STUFFED INTO ONE OF THE ARMS

Other Seals and Shapes You May Find Useful for Including in Poppets

1. **Chaldean Commanding Sigil:** From the outside in, the seven winds, followed by the seven stars (planets, their sigils and names), and the seven ruling angels. This seal comes from the Picatrix. Write your intention in the center of the disk.

2. **The Triangle:** Often used to contain power or separate a particular energy from other energies in the working. Also symbolizes the cone of power and the point of manifestation.

3. **Alchemical Seal:** Use the alchemical seal for personal transformation.

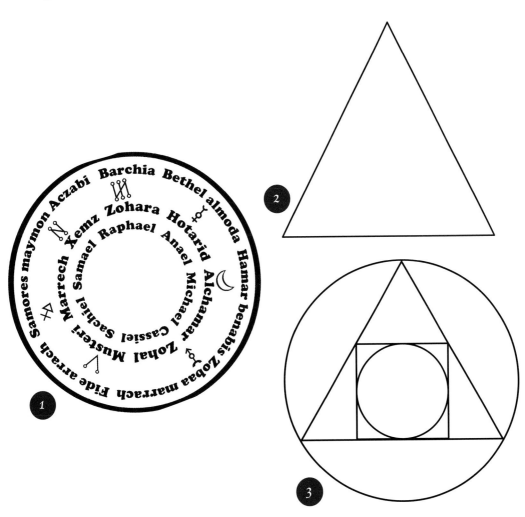

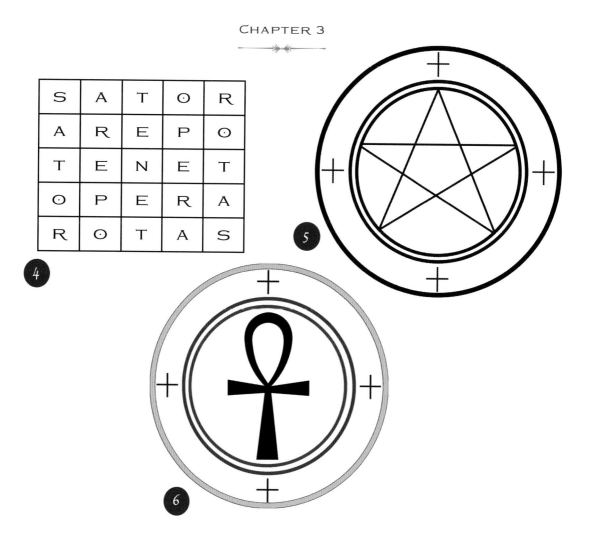

4. **SATOR Square:** This is used for protection, banishing, destroying inflammation and disease, and defeating gossip. It can also be used effectively as a spoken command, particularly if you recite with great feeling and conviction.

5. **The Pentacle:** This is used for protection and accessing the powers of earth, air, fire, water, and the human ability of manipulating thought into form. The circle represents the Spirit of the Universe—the perfection of divinity. The pentacle is a representation of the path of the planet Venus in the heavens.

6. **The Egyptian Ankh:** A sigil used for a variety of purposes, including petitions at the gates of death for those who are very sick and ready to cross over (this works for animals as well as people). The ankh is life-affirming in that it is used for good health, strength, a fruitful manifestation of wealth, birth of people and animals, long life, knowledge, and protection.

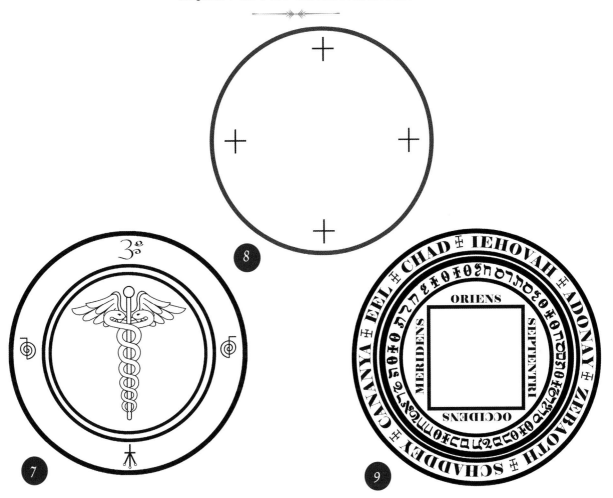

7. **Healer's Sigil:** Uses the caduceus (center), OM (top—the sound of perfection), the Reiki Double Cho-Ku-Rei (right and left—the gateway to manifestation), and the Reiki Harth (bottom sigil—healing of the heart and personal enlightenment). Use this sigil for any healing work. Also applicable to spiritual knowledge.

8. **The Crossroads Seal:** Works for all manner of petitions. Write your intent inside the circle. Dot each equal-armed cross with a magickal oil of your choice.

9. **The Spirit Circle:** The spirit circle summons the names of God and the four directions. This general spirit circle is from the Sixth and Seventh Books of Moses.

10. **The Runic Spider Web Circle**: Used to capture and hold any energy. Burn to manifest or bury whole to catch a criminal or evil person in their own web of deceit.

11. **Love Poppet Sigil**: Words written in shapes are thought to carry more power. Using a heart shape touches the universal idea of love and can go to the "heart" of the matter.

12. **Eyes of Spirit Sigil**: Used for planetary workings, invoking the wisdom of Spirit or angelic energy, finding the truth of a matter, or protecting a person or object; also known as the angelic wheel of power.

13. **Hexefus/Blummersterne**: Flower of protective power! The Blummersterne symbol means "flower star" and is used in Pennsylvania Dutch lore to ward off bad luck, accidents, illness, gossip, and general evil. The symbol is invoked as a protective sigil for home, barn, office, or vehicle and works well in healing magick. The Blummersterne is also called the Hexefus rosette, meaning "witch's foot."

11

Passion, the gift of joy the epitome of harmony now and forever, I conjure thee O powers of love so that you will bring to me the fire

12

Alpha Omega

13

Closing the Poppet

Closing the poppet can be a small magickal rite in itself. You might light a match and quickly extinguish it inside the poppet to add the "fire of spirit" or use a different technique of activation, such as drawing a specific sigil or rune over the poppet. You can blow into the poppet right before stitching it up, bidding it once again to be of service in the way you choose and reminding the poppet it can only function as you have commanded. You may wish to have a specific chant that you always use when finishing the last of your stitching or when making the mouth of a clay poppet, or you might like to pass a particular scent of incense over the work. The more unique the rite, with layers of specific thought and action, the better, because in this small technique lies a locking mechanism that only you know.

Basic Construction of the Traditional Cotton Poppet

1. Using a pencil, trace the outline of the poppet onto the cotton. This example uses traditional unbleached muslin. When selecting bleached or unbleached muslin (or any fabric choice), feel the weight of the fabric between your fingers. If the cloth is too thin, it will easily fray and tear during the construction process. Select a fabric of heavier weight.

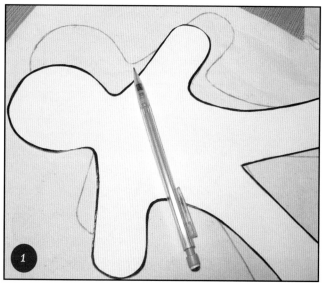

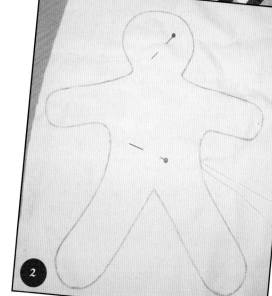

2. There are two types of openings for stuffing used in traditional cotton poppets. The primitive opening (where a slit is cut in the back of the poppet after the stitching is completed) and the side opening (where space is left unsewn). The primitive opening is used for easier stuffing. The side opening is a bit more complicated, particularly with its placement. It shouldn't be too close to a bend in the stitching line (such as between the legs or on curves under the arms) because it can make the poppet difficult to stuff and to close.

3. Normally, a side opening is much smaller, giving rise to problems in stuffing, particularly if you need to place large roots, charms, or other objects into the poppet. However, if you plan to insert only a few herbs, one small charm, or a slip of paper, you might like to use this type of opening instead. The primitive opening is often used so that the basic seams look clean and unmarred and there is plenty of room to add ingredients.

4. If you choose to use the primitive opening technique, sew entirely along the pencil line. Trim the seams to ¼ or ½ inch, depending on how much of a folded edge you want when the doll is turned. Clip corners, being careful not to cut the stitching. Clipping the corners and circular or rounded seams allows the material to "give" a bit during stuffing, letting your curved seams fill and smooth out without puckering.

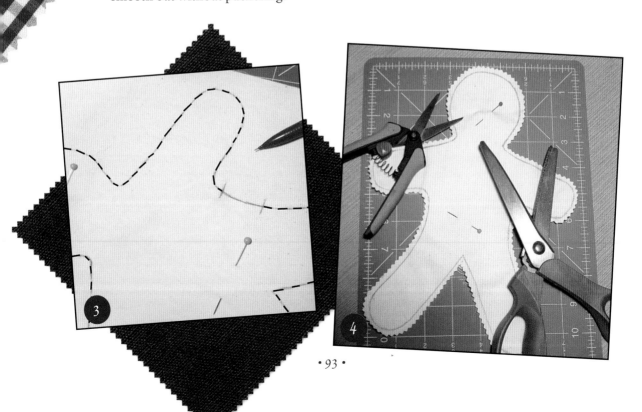

5. After the seams are trimmed and clipped, draw a straight line with a pencil on one side of the poppet. Make sure the line isn't too long or too short. Too long and the seam can fray and be difficult to close. Too short and you won't have enough room to add your spell ingredients.

6. Once you have drawn the line, gently pull the front material from the back material. This can be a bit tricky on a smaller poppet size—just take your time.

7. The next step is to cut along the pencil line with a pair of sharp scissors, being careful not to clip the bottom fabric. You are only clipping the top piece of fabric.

8. Turn poppet right-side out. Your poppet is now ready for stuffing.

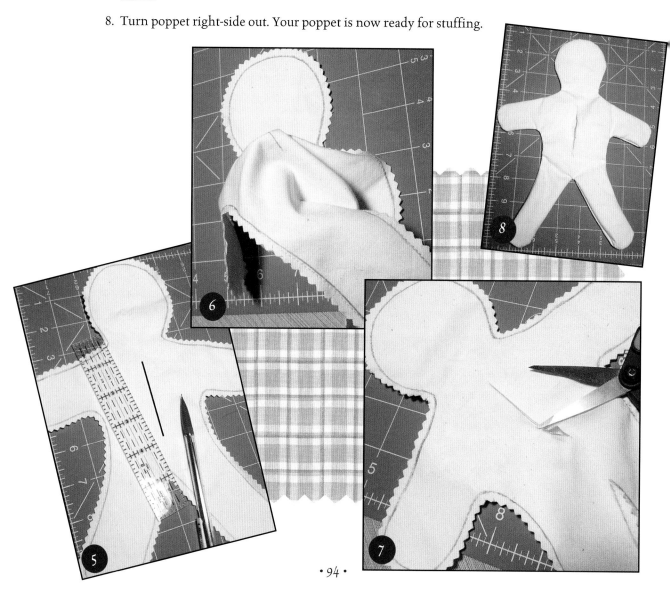

9. If you choose the side-opening style of the poppet, stitch along the pencil line, leaving the marked area open. Strengthen stitching at edges of opening by reversing a few stitches on either side.

10. As with the primitive opening poppet, trim seams and clip curves, except this time you are going to leave a "tag" when trimming the poppet. The tag makes it easier to close the stuffed poppet and helps to create a neater seam.

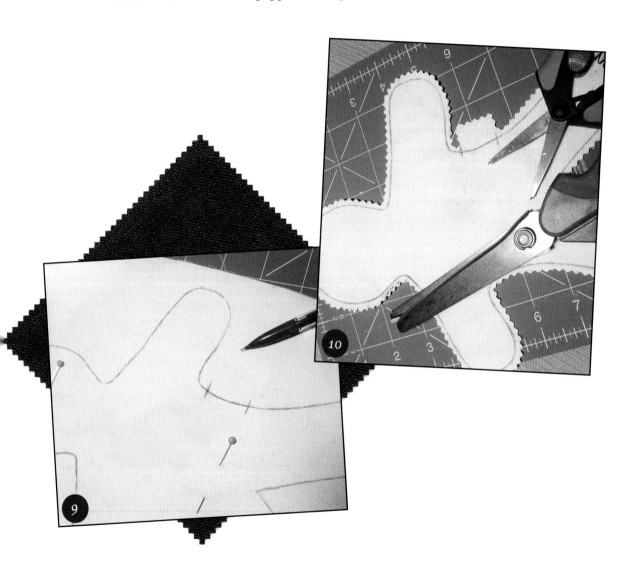

11. Turn the poppet right-side out and tuck the tag inside the body of the poppet. Your doll is ready for stuffing.

12. Stuff the poppet. Add any spell-related items, such as pictures, sigils, or other inclusions.

13. Remember to command the poppet to match your intent before stitching up the back or side of the poppet.

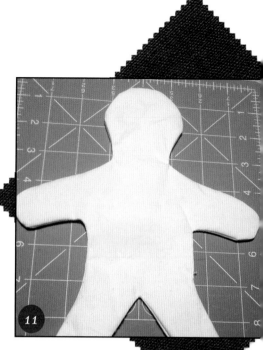

Should you wish to write your petition in permanent marker on the doll, you may like to take the following words from the Picatrix into consideration:

> You ought to write the name of the Lord of the Mansion* and your petition with it. In those images that are made for the good, and to cause gathering, uniting and generating friendship and love, you ought to write on the chest of the figure; and in all workings that are done to cause disunion, separation and to generate enmity and ill will, you ought to write behind the shoulders (that is, along the spine of the image); while in all workings that are done to acquire glory, honor, and advancement, you ought to write on the head of that image (Greer and Warnock 2010, 295).

*There are several differing resources regarding the mansions of the moon: the Picatrix (mentioned above) and H. C. Agrippa's *Occult Philosophy*. Another excellent resource is *The Complete Magician's Tables* by Stephen Skinner. You may find this website helpful: http://www.yeatsvision.com/mansions.html. To find which mansion is currently active for timing the making or birthing of poppets, you can use an astrological software program or purchase an app for your phone or iPad: https://itunes.apple.com/us/app/mansions-of-the-moon/id479654763?mt=8.

To increase the power of your poppet, you might also take into consideration the planetary hours or other astrological information. You may find my book *The Witching Hour* useful in timing the creation and birthing of your cloth poppet.

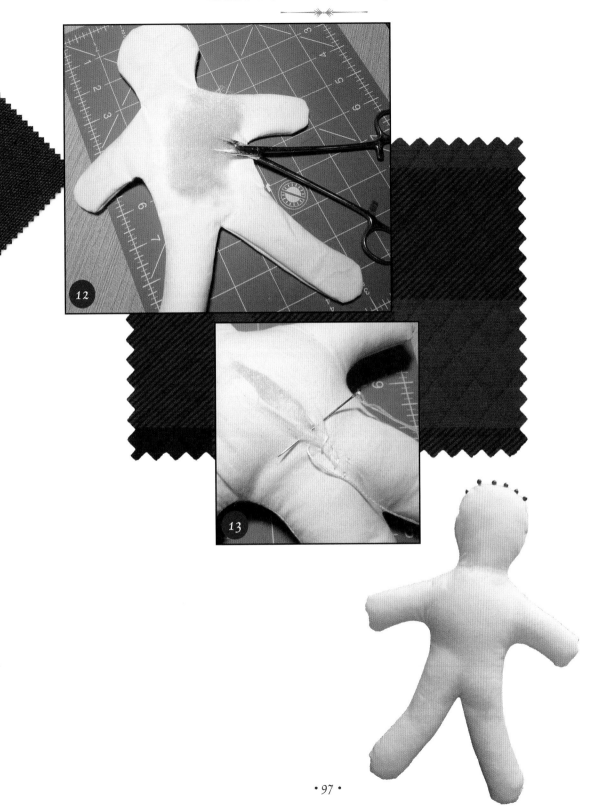

HISTORICALLY POPPETS WERE USED AS "FUTURE"
DEVICES, ENCOURAGING SOMETHING TO
HAPPEN THAT HAD NOT YET OCCURRED

Pins, Sticks, and Nails in Poppets

Folks have been poking sticks, nails, and pins (or drilling holes) in poppets since the magick of ancient Egypt, Greece, and Rome. The pointed vehicle (such as a pin or nail) denoted the direction of concentrated energy and was used to "nail down" the energy into the doll. Surprisingly enough, most poppets in the ancient world weren't designed to kill people—instead, they were fashioned to deflect or defeat. In many cases, they were used in future tense, urging the doll to make something happen (or not). Using a doll for revenge of a past injustice was not common; rather, the force of the doll was directed to the future, whether it was stopping a person from doing more harm, winning a chariot race, or getting away with a crime.

Judicial poppets (those used for court proceedings) were common—not against the criminal, but against the counsel! In several instances, attorneys claimed they lost their cases because their tongues had been tied by magick. When working on legal issues, I teach my students to concentrate on attorney action and judge's decisions (that the client will be treated fairly and without duress), not the individual who is accusing the defendant. In the realm of poppet magick, the past is the past—it is the future you must change.

In the realm of poppet magick, the past is the past— it is the future you must change.

For example, let's say you wanted to do a protection poppet because Harold has been giving you a really bad time at work. You would make a poppet to represent Harold and inside the poppet include a taglock (something that belongs to him, such as a pencil, a business card, etc.; if you didn't have any of those things, you might write his name nine times on a piece of paper). Then, you might hold the doll so that your breath hits the doll and intone the following chant nine times:

You can't see me
You can't hear me
You can't hurt me anymore.

While repeating the chant, you would stick a pin through both of the poppet's eyes, one pin through his ears, and one through his mouth (or you could sew his mouth shut). If the situation is really bad, you might also bind his arms and legs with wire or strong string. This act is not to physically hurt Harold—basically, it is to shut him up, push his attention elsewhere, and keep him from harming you or anyone else. Finally, you might perform the sending technique in chapter 4 to finish the job.

Another way to deal with a bothersome person is to make the poppet, and, in ritual, bind the poppet to the earth by sticking a knife through it and into the earth outdoors (where no one will bother it). This act is not to kill the individual, it is to give that person to the earth for positive self-transformation. Of course, if you stuck the poppet in a graveyard…um…don't forget the rule of three: what you put out comes back to thee.

Pins, sticks, and nails were also used to direct energy in a positive way. For example, some practitioners use straight pins inserted at chakra points on the doll to direct healing energy. Most of my dolls carry pins of some type as well as unique needles. I have several styles and combinations for different purposes. In Braucherei work we use safety pins both for protection and to "pin" an area of the body that needs healing focus. Safety pins can also be used to affix a small petition of healing right onto the doll. This is particularly useful for family poppets, where you might have made a poppet for each member of the family. Life changes, so your requests for them will change. Placing the petition on the outside of the doll allows you to remove it when necessary. In Braucherei straight, sharp objects (such as nails, screws, stakes, and straight pins) are used in banishing and pinning the evil created by the individual back on him or her. Some of these directive sharp objects are long doll needles decorated with beads, rawhide, jute, polymer clay, painted gears, glass eyes, watch faces, and more. These long needles have been turned into very powerful dollies in their own right! The safety pin is used for healing, directing energy, protection, and holding petitions. Charms or pieces of colored thread are often tied or secured with jump rings to the safety pin for a variety of magickal purposes.

Charm pins can be added to your puppets and spirit dolls to increase the connection to your intent. I learned to use safety pins as magical vehicles from Preston Zerby in the early 90s. Preston taught me several Braucherei techniques. He always wore a safety pin on his left sleeve indicating that this was to keep away evil and witches. In Preston's view, witches were people who carried negativity in their hearts or they were individuals who willingly would try to harm him. The Pennsylvania Dutch understanding of the word "Witch" is not the same as those who practice the religion of Witchcraft today.

Safety pins were also pinned over the heart to bring good fortune or true love. For example, those who sold goods at market would pray over the pins and then fix them to their shirt or blouse in hopes of having a good business day, "pinning" good fortune to their family or career.

The photograph shows possible embellishments, including charms and beads for your safety pin enchantments. Undecorated safety pins are an innocuous way of carrying empowered objects with you, as they can be pinned to the inside or hem of a garment and no one would ever be the wiser.

four

POPPET RITUALS

Birthing, Naming, Sending, and Deactivating Rituals

Once your poppet is completed, you may wish to employ a birthing and naming ritual to bind and solidify the doll's purpose. It is thought that if the doll "rests" for a period of three days, buried in the earth or lain across a cauldron of blessed water that is changed each day, the energies will coalesce in a stronger pattern. The first two rituals provided are the longer version of the birthing process that includes resting the doll for three days; they are what I use for virtually every poppet I make. However, time is not always on your side—you may need to put a poppet together and birth it quickly. The third ritual, entitled Fast Track Poppet Birthing Ritual, can fulfill this need.

THIS GUARDIAN DOLLY, OR WARNING/WATCHING DOLL, IS
FILLED WITH GRAVE DIRT FROM MY ANCESTORS' GRAVES;
SEE CHAPTER 5 FOR FURTHER INSTRUCTION

Dirt Birthing and Naming Ritual Formula

For this ritual, first gather dirt taken from a peaceful place (not a cemetery)—enough to fill a small container. The dirt must be completely dry. Place in full sun or on a cookie sheet in the oven at the lowest setting for at least one hour to ensure the dirt is dry.

Then gather the following:

- 3 tablespoons dirt from the entrance of a cemetery (for protective purposes) or 3 tablespoons dirt from an ancestor's grave (in either case, use dirt that has been ritually taken—where prayers were given and an offering was left)

- 3 tablespoons dirt from a hallowed place

- 1 cup blessed and empowered basil

- 9 drops holy water

If your intuition tells you to omit the dirt from the cemetery, that is fine; always follow your gut feelings. Ritually cleanse and bless the dirt as you did your supplies. Then pass your hand over the dirt in a counterclockwise direction, saying the following nine times:

In the name of _____ (insert the name of your divinity),
I conjure and command thee, O earth, to be the womb of creation.
I bless thee in the name of the seven angels.
I bless thee in the name of the seven stars.
I bless thee in the name of the seven planets.
I bless thee in the name of the seven winds.

Make a hole in the dirt large enough for the doll. Intone the following conjuration nine times, blowing into the dirt after each repetition:

In the name of _____ (insert the name of your divinity),
I empower and command thee in the name of the seven angels.
I empower and command thee in the name of the seven stars.
I empower and command thee in the name of the seven planets.
I empower and command thee in the name of the seven winds
That thou shalt do my bidding; I know thee will do this for me!

Wrap the poppet in white muslin (to keep it clean), and bury it in the dirt. On the surface of the dirt, draw an equal-armed cross. Cover the pot with a lid or a piece of black cloth. Leave the doll in the dirt for three days. On the dawn of the fourth day, open the pot and intone the following nine times:

> By the power of (insert the name of your divinity),
> I raise thee in the name of the seven angels.
> I raise thee in the name of the seven stars.
> I raise thee in the name of the seven planets.
> I raise thee in the name of the seven winds
> That thou shalt do my bidding; I know thee will do this for me!

At the end of the ninth repetition, ceremoniously lift the doll from the dirt, blow on where the mouth is (or would be), and name it, saying:

> In the name of (your divinity),
> Thou art (person's name or energy pattern,
> such as "healing" or "prosperity") to me!
> I command that thou art born unto this world to do my bidding!

Repeat three times. Then say:

> As above, so below—it shall be so!
> I know thee will do this for me.

Sprinkle three drops of holy water on the head of the doll. Draw an equal-armed cross in the air three times over the poppet. Finish with:

> This working is sealed.

Note: Never give a poppet a living person's name unless you intend to use the doll in 27 days, which is a Braucherei/Whisper Magick cycle of completion. The number 27 factors down to 9 (2 + 7), which is reduced to 3—the number of charming. An unattended "named" doll has been known to wreak havoc in the life of the doll maker—just like a puppy, it gets bored easily! Do not leave a named doll lying around with nothing to do! I actually give my "in process" dolls toys, magickal items, crystals, flowers, jewelry, etc., to keep them busy if I have to leave them for any length of time before their completion. I may have nine or ten dolls on my work table at any given moment, so

I designed special bags to store them. These bags are decorated with "holding" sigils (such as the Eyes of Spirit sigil in chapter 3) to keep the dolls' energy safely confined. Wrapping the doll in a black cloth can be just as effective—it is all in what you choose to do.

Your doll is now ready for a spell or ritual work, or you can simply command the doll immediately using your initial intention statement or by using the sending technique given later in this chapter. If you command the doll immediately, be sure to seal your statement by drawing an equal-armed cross in the air over the doll to seal your final intent.

Water Birthing Ritual

The water birthing and naming ritual is much like that of the dirt with only a few changes. The formula for the water is:

One mason jar of holy water or a ritual pot with blessed water with either three pinches of salt or the inclusion of fresh or dried herbs such as rosemary, hyssop, or lavender (or all three).

You can also put the doll in a dry, empty jar, cap it, and set the jar in a stream or creek (should you have one close by). However, the doll must stay there at least twenty-four hours or three days at best. If the doll is to bind a criminal, you can place the jar in stagnant water for three days. Light a white candle. Say:

In the name of (your divinity), fire sparks the waters of life!

Plunge the lit candle into the water. (Note: Candle can not be reused. Discard after the ceremony.) Pass your hand over the water in a counterclockwise direction, saying nine times:

In the name of (insert the name of your divinity),
I conjure and command thee, O water, to be the womb of creation.
I bless thee in the name of the seven angels.
I bless thee in the name of the seven stars.
I bless thee in the name of the seven planets.
I bless thee in the name of the seven winds.

Intone the following conjuration nine times, blowing into the water after each repetition:

> In the name of (insert the name of your divinity),
> I empower and command thee in the name of the seven angels.
> I empower and command thee in the name of the seven stars.
> I empower and command thee in the name of the seven planets.
> I empower and command thee in the name of the seven winds
> That thou shalt do my bidding; I know thee will do this for me.

Position the doll over the rim of the open jar (being careful it doesn't get wet). Drape a black cloth over the doll and the jar, then draw an equal-armed cross in the air over the black cloth.

Repeat this ceremony for three days each morning, as the water and the salt or herbs must be changed every day.

On the dawn of the fourth day, remove the black cloth from the doll and intone the following nine times:

> By the power of (insert the name of your divinity),
> I raise thee in the name of the seven angels.
> I raise thee in the name of the seven stars.
> I raise thee in the name of the seven planets.
> I raise thee in the name of the seven winds.
> By my command, thou shalt do my bidding;
> I know thee will do this for me!

At the end of the ninth repetition, ceremoniously lift the doll from the rim of the jar, sprinkle some of the water on the poppet, blow on where the mouth is (or would be), and name it, saying:

> In the name of (your divinity),
> Thou art (person's name or energy pattern, such as "healing" or "prosperity") to me!
> Thou art born unto this world to do my bidding!

Repeat three times. Then say:

> As above, so below; it shall be so.
> I know thee will do this for me!

You can sprinkle some of the water onto the doll if you like, then draw an equal-armed cross in the air over the poppet three times, saying:

This working is sealed.

Your doll is now ready for spell or ritual work, or you can simply command the doll immediately using your initial intention statement. If you command the doll immediately, be sure to seal your statement by drawing an equal-armed cross in the air over the doll to seal your final intent.

Fast Track Poppet Birthing Ritual

There might be times when you will need to birth and name a poppet quickly—perhaps there is an emergency or your schedule is so packed, you only have a very small window of opportunity. You may also feel that since you have added your intent while constructing the doll, a quick birthing is all that is needed.

Hold the poppet in both hands and face east, the place of birth. Silently connect with Spirit or utter a prayer or incantation of your choice. Begin chanting the word "air" nine times, making sure your breath floats across the doll. Feel the element of air enter the field of the doll.

Chant the word "fire" nine times, again making sure your breath floats across the doll. In your mind see sparks of fire surrounding the doll and then melting into the doll.

Chant the word "water" nine times, letting your breath roll across the poppet. Envision the element of water filling the field of the doll and gently melting into the image.

Chant the word "earth" nine times. With the "earth" word, the power of the doll descends to the earth plane. In your mind, see the doll connected with the person for which it is intended. Imagine an invisible cord that snakes out from the poppet and into the visualization of the living individual to which it is connected.

Next, chant the word "spirit" nine times. This is where all the elements coalesce and become the spirit of the doll. It can also be a blessing from Spirit, that beautiful energy that carries love throughout the universe. When you feel the energy around the doll pulsing in your hands, begin chanting:

In the name of (say your chosen divinity), you are (the person's name).

You can also say "I lock thee to (the person's name)" while running the energy up from the earth to the top of your head, then down into your heart chakra and out into your hands and the doll. You could also run the energy down from the heavens into your crown chakra, down to your toes, then back up to your heart chakra and out into your arms and hands. Or you can run energy from the ground up with the first chant, and then from the heavens down on the second chant, followed by ground up on the third and heaven down on the fourth until you have completed nine times of chanting "In the name of _____, you are _____" or "I lock thee to (the person's name)."

Lift the doll in the air. Say:

> (Name of the poppet), thou art born unto this world to do my bidding.
> I command thee to live! I command thee to manifest my desire!

Blow into the poppet's mouth three times. Then say:

> As above, so below; it shall be so. I know thee will do this for me!

Finish by drawing an equal-armed cross in the air over the belly of the doll three times to seal the birthing. At this point, you can direct the doll what to do or declare "This working is sealed!" and save the doll to command it later.

Please understand that this is only one way to quickly birth the poppet and that you can enhance or change the meaning and power of the elements as you chant. Activating a poppet is highly personal, and you should feel absolutely comfortable with what you are doing. You can also expand this ritual by adding physical representations of the elements and passing them over the poppet as you chant. This is a highly effective way to empower the work and takes about fifteen minutes of your time from start to finish. You may also like to take portions of the longer rituals (earth or water) and add them to this one. The choice is up to you.

Poppets in Magick

Goddesses that lend their energy well to poppet/spirit doll construction include Norse Dame Holda, Frigg, and the Norns; Greek Hecate, Athena, Aphrodite, and Arachne; Egyptian Neith, Isis, and Bast; Japanese Shinto sun goddess Amaterasu; Cherokee Kanene Ski Amai Yehi, and any divinity that is concerned with domestic affairs (as in spinning, weaving, or sewing). Your first poppet may be styled to serve or represent one of these goddesses in an effort to celebrate the energy of creating poppets and dolls through the assistance of divinity. Such a poppet might be honored in ceremony and receive monthly or weekly offerings.

Once you have completed and birthed your poppet, it is ready for meditation, ritual, spellwork, or sending (where the doll is commanded to reach out into the universe and perform a specific task). To send a poppet is to make it work—to call it to action and tell it what to do when, where, and how.

The ceremonies in which you use your poppet can be as ornate or as simple as you desire. Many people talk to their poppets, particularly if they are of the long-term nature such as a poppet dedicated to a goddess, good health, or prosperity. In this chapter I provided three birthing rituals that can lead directly into sending the poppet. Alternatively, you can make the poppet, birth it, and then let it rest in a box, wrapped in cloth or a bag, until you are ready to send it.

To send a poppet is to tell it what to do when, where, and how. Make it work. Call it to action!

*I*t ain't over till it's over!
Do not let events or circumstances
that may appear to be the conclusion
actually be the conclusion.

Sending the Poppet

In this photo we see the three-headed poppet, primarily used to separate a negative group mind, asking for peace and loving transformation in its place. As you can see, the format using the rune candleboard and the colors of red, white, and black along with the symbol of Thor's hammer fall in the realm of Norse magick. The goose feather is an offering to Dame Holda, the goddess of the Wild Hunt and protectress of children. When I send a poppet, I try to stay within the realm of the system I am working. If I petition the Norse/Germanic gods and goddesses, then all the correspondences I choose are related to them. I am a firm believer in not mixing systems unless what you are asking for supersedes the points where the systems do not agree. For example, in asking for divine love—a pure and compassionate vibration in itself, a perfection of divine energy at its highest manifestation—the request trumps deity/spirit squabbles.

The primary force in sending a poppet lies within you. You must "know" that what you are doing will work and what you are asking for will come to pass. If you have any doubt, there is a good chance that the process of change will either fail or flow in a direction you didn't see. Some people use a divinatory tool to check the direction of their sending before the actual ritual to ensure their feelings match their intent. Your spellwork should be mentally calm, performed with the conviction that all will be as you say, and you must not waver in your thoughts, should the first few events after the working appear to be at cross-purposes to your desire. Hold onto the "knowledge" that in the end it will be done as you say. I teach my students that it ain't over till it's over! Do not let events or circumstances that may appear to be the conclusion actually be the conclusion. Do not give up just because you hear something about a situation. Our world is fraught with gossip, misinformation, and misleading, twisted pseudo-evidence that can tangle, trip, and hobble the mind. Remember: it ain't over till it's over!

If the work carries subconscious guilt, fear, or you know in your heart that what you are requesting is immoral, cruel, or downright wrong, the magick will turn back, and, like the bite and squeeze of the adder of justice, you will pay dearly.

Many of the spellworking patterns we use today stem from the ancient Chaldeans, Egyptians, Greeks, and Romans. For example, ritual purification of one's self and the area in which you choose to do magickal work, the petitioning of deity as in "in the name of _____" at the beginning of a spell formula, using an analogy to click that "knowing" in your mind ("as a cadaver lies cold and useless, so wilt lies against me have no power"), and the disposal of spell elements (in tombs, wells, rivers, or caves) all date back to the ancient practitioners. Likewise, whisper magick (the combination of Braucherei and Granny enchantments) and the absolute adherence to secrecy are also ancient elements. For example, in ancient Greece Apollo's priest uttered his famous curse along the seashore only after he was out of earshot of the enemy ships; Pelops waited until he was alone on the beach in the dead of night to urge Poseidon to bind his enemy; and Orestes kept his words under his breath to turn back a curse (Faraone and Obbink 1991, 17). Secrecy is a science and a tactic not to be ignored.

Items used in sending a poppet are employed for a variety of reasons, including

- to heighten or help solidify the practitioner's mood, imbuing self-confidence and that feeling of certainty necessary for a victorious end result. If the scent of patchouli does it for you, then that is what you choose.

- to access the power of the various levels of the vibrational universe, such as a particular choice of color, aroma, shape, or energy function (fire burns as well as lights, etc.).

- tradition—although I don't always agree with this. Actions can become petrified, morphing into tradition erroneously, often because the original practitioner didn't know the science and based their success solely on something innocuous or odd, which became a tradition. On the other hand, actions of tradition can help to bind or solidify a group mind. Always know why you use a traditional act or object, and understand its purpose in the matrix of your own working. In this way, tradition will aid rather than hamper the working. Choose your balance.

Sending your doll can be done in a magick circle, in sacred space, or in a spiritual place (such as the woods or a place where you connect with Spirit and have a feeling of well-being). Some practitioners utter prayers rather than physically create a sacred area—what works for you is what is right for you. Don't be afraid to try sending in various ways. Eventually, you will choose a way that will always work for you—this is a combination of you and your environment that will create the proper mindset for success. A sending can be long or short.

IN THIS WORKING, THE DOLL REPRESENTS A GODDESS AND HAS
BEEN USED MORE THAN ONCE FOR VARIOUS PETITIONS. HERE
THE PAPER SIGIL WILL BE FOLDED, ANOINTED, AND PINNED TO
THE DOLL'S BELLY WITH A SAFETY PIN. THE GOLDEN COINS WILL
BE DISTRIBUTED AS ITEMS OF GOOD LUCK TO VARIOUS PEOPLE.
THE CRYSTAL BOOSTED THE POWER, AND THE CAULRON FILLED
WITH BLESSED WATER REPRESENTS THE BIRTH OF THE SPELL.

Easy Steps for Sending Your Poppet

1. Breathe deeply three times to clear the mind and connect to Spirit and the potential of the universe all around you.

2. Light a candle to represent that the sending has begun or light incense to open the way to Spirit and raise your personal vibrations.

3. Invoke deity or universal power.

4. State your intent clearly.

5. Bless the doll with a bit of oil and liquid fluid condenser that matches your intent.

6. Whisper your intent into the doll as you hold it, running energy up through the ground to the top of your head and then out into your hands and into the doll.

7. Add a chant to build power. In Braucherei chants must be said nine times. As you chant, your breath should always flow over the poppet. It is here where a pin, nail, or safety pin can be used to direct power into the doll.

8. Whisper into the doll's mouth or ears (whatever feels right) exactly what you want it to do. Through the mouth, the energy would travel down through the heart chakra and into the "root" of the doll.

9. Intone a final sending statement that matches your intent. "In the name of (divinity name), I command you, poppet (or poppet's name), to go forth and do not rest until you have _____ (fill in the blank)."

10. Seal the work. I use an equal-armed cross drawn in the air over the poppet three times.

11. Enact the final disposition of the doll. Will you burn it immediately in a fire-safe cauldron? Will you place it upon a soft bed to send dreams of information or healing energy to a friend? Do you plan to release the poppet in the river? Bury it in the earth? Place it on the railroad tracks? (Hey, it can happen). How you dispose of the doll in respect to the sending and the work is just as important as how you created it in the first place.

12. If you have invoked a deity or a universal power, now is the time to offer thanks and perhaps an offering specific to that deity, spirit, or power.

You will know by your feelings when the sending process has concluded.

Deactivating or Decommissioning a Poppet

If your desire has been met and your poppet was of temporary intent, it is time to deactivate or decommission the working. You may also wish to deactivate a poppet that is old, choosing to replace it with a new one. Either way, you should release the energy with as much care as you constructed it. To do this, you may wish to cast a magick circle, recite a favorite prayer, or intone a particular chant before the deactivation so that you are working in sacred space. Then, begin by circling your hand in a clockwise direction nine times over the poppet, saying:

> By the power of _____ (insert divinity or planetary power name here),
> I release and disperse thee in the name of the seven angels.
> I release and disperse thee in the name of the seven stars.
> I release and disperse thee in the name of the seven planets.
> I release and disperse thee in the name of the seven winds.
> I thank thee for thy service. Now your work is done.
> I command that you go in joy and peace.

Continue reciting the same verse eight more times as you take apart the poppet. When the poppet is thoroughly dismantled, burn what you can outdoors and dispose of the rest off of your property.

Please note that in this book, clockwise and counterclockwise motion are reversed and may not be what you are normally used to. The technique where counterclockwise is used to draw something to you and clockwise is used to expel was employed by Sybil Leek. If you are not comfortable with this mechanic, feel free to change it to suit your needs.

five

A PLETHORA of POPPETS

Working with Various Mediums

Clay, rock, birdseed, salt—all these and more can be molded into a magickal poppet. We'll explore various mediums in this chapter.

Working with Clay

Clay provides a marvelous blend of thought and action, allowing you to easily manipulate the energy field of the doll. Done in sacred space, the power of the poppet begins to grow as the shape takes form. You can listen to music, burn a scented candle or incense, and let your mind and fingers work together in beautiful synergy. Many people worry about their skill when it comes to fashioning a clay poppet and fear that if the doll doesn't look like a particular person, then it won't work. This isn't the case. I've found that your skill level is not an issue; it is your intent and how you employ the energy that is important. Many practitioners talk to their poppets while they are making them, whispering chants and charms associated with the intent, as well as addressing the poppet by name. In this book I've used polymer clay, as I've found it to be the most easily manipulated. When the finished item is placed in an oven, the polymer hardens and retains its shape.

A polymer clay poppet doesn't have to be baked; there are times when you will want the clay to be malleable throughout the intended spellwork. If you don't whip the poppet over your head (unless you want to), it should stay together without baking until your working is finished. Since polymer clay is a plastic compound that won't rot, you may not want to bury it, and it shouldn't be burned due to caustic fumes. Once baked, wherever you put it, it will stay there without disintegrating. It can, however, be broken, which works well in spells where you wish to break negativity or disease.

While massaging the clay to make it workable, I often add magickal oils, a very tiny amount of liquid fluid condenser, and herbal powders—not too much, as the clay may not adhere properly or it may crack before the poppet is completed. With today's array of beautiful clay colors, you can choose the perfect match for your intent.

The partially completed red poppet shown at the beginning of the chapter is for drawing love, so I chose a fire-engine-colored clay, added orange blossom oil, a touch

I USUALLY BEGIN CONSTRUCTING CLAY
POPPETS WITH SMALL, BASIC SHAPES

of rose oil, and powdered rose petals mixed with a bit of sugar. If you plan to bake the poppet, be careful how much sugar you add because sugar burns. Only a tiny bit is necessary. I always make a hole for the navel as a ritual representation of the poppet's connection to the earth plane.

Although some practitioners like to form their poppet out of one large ball of clay, I usually begin with small, basic shapes—a ball for the head and rounded rectangles for the body, legs, and arms. I use a clay cutter to slice two tubes in half (one for the legs and one for the arms).

The black poppet is a sin eater, designed to absorb negativity that enters the home or the office. The black represents the void, or the still point from which all things are birthed or transformed. I created a cavity in the poppet's head to hold a tiny amethyst crystal and angelica, frankincense, myrrh, and rosemary herbs.

I DESIGNED THIS POPPET IN A SITTING POSITION SO THAT IT CAN
PERCH ON A DESK OR RIGHT ON TOP OF A COMPUTER TOWER

You can shape your poppet's image in any way you desire.

FINISHED CLAY LOVE POPPET WITH COPPER
WIRE HAIR AND BLACK BRADS FOR EYES

Once I have all the pieces rolled, cut, and ready to form, I work on the face. I try to get the expression to match my intent. With the love doll above, I wanted him to be happy—after all, he's found the love of his life! The sin eater holds a different expression. If you are having trouble smoothing the body parts together, you can insert toothpicks for more stability. As shown here, your poppet doesn't have to be in the prone (gingerbread) position; you can shape the image in any way you desire.

For oven-baked clays, you might like to try a binding liquid such as Liquid Sculpey that solidifies during the baking process, ensuring that all the body parts will stay together. The liquid binder can also be used to hold embellishments during the baking process. Plastic, cloth, and paper embellishments will not normally survive the oven and have to be glued on after the piece has cooled. Glass beads, however, normally take the heat without issue.

Additional embellishments to the love poppet shown here include coil wire for hair and black brads inserted into the eye cavities. These items were metal so I could add them before baking the doll. The sin eater has several amethyst chips that were added with the binding liquid before baking.

(ABOVE) THIS POPPET WAS CONSTRUCTED USING A SERIES OF ROLLED CLAY PIECES

(RIGHT) FINISHED SIN EATER POPPET HOLDING AN AMETHYST CHIP

Although clay poppets can be strikingly beautiful to behold, I've found the more unusual the doll, the odder it is—and the more unique it becomes. Neither the love poppet nor the sin eater will win any art contests or beauty pageants for dolls; they will, however, perform their function quite well.

Seven-Herb Color Dolls

Over the years I have formulated several recipes for clay and wax poppets that friends and family have requested for specific needs. After choosing a color of clay to match the individual's personality, I then create a spirit dolly to help them heal or change in a positive way. To choose the color of the clay, sit quietly and think of that individual. Say quietly: "Mind to mind, heart to heart, soul to soul. Reveal thy needed color to me." The first color that comes to mind is the color you should use. Sometimes you will see the person in your mind's eye bathed in a specific color; sometimes you won't see anything. Don't panic. Try the request again. If nothing comes to you, choose a different type of magick. The seven-herb color doll is not suitable for their needs.

I don't take a lot of time to mold this image—it roughly looks like a person, although sometimes it looks like something from another galaxy—whatever! The point is that the doll is to work for the individual in a positive way. As I create the doll, I massage the seven herbs directly into the clay, adding a touch of magickal oil and usually ten drops of liquid universal fluid condenser. When the doll is nearly finished, I take a bamboo skewer and create an opening in the doll from the top of the head to the feet (being careful to not punch through the feet). This cavity can be filled with additional herbs and a sigil or petition in the fashion of Franz Bardon and the creation of his "elementaries" (see Bardon 1956). When you have inserted the desired material, seal the opening and proceed with the normal birthing procedure for the doll.

When the difficulty, problem, issue, or circumstance has passed out of their lives, I instruct them to break the doll (to break their connection to the doll) and then burn the pieces.

Seven-Herb Insomnia Dolly: Vervain, dill, violet fragrance and flowers, chamomile, thyme, rosemary, woodruff

Seven-Herb Weight Loss Dolly: Buckthorn, ivy, nettle, sassafras, St. John's wort, celery seed, birch bark

Seven-Herb Stop Smoking Dolly: Catnip, hyssop, peppermint, angelica, cohosh (black or blue), echinacea, hot peppers

Seven-Herb Surgery/Wound Healing Dolly: Vervain, chamomile, dandelion, flax seed, lemon peel, onion peel, marigold

Seven-Herb Money Dolly: (for emergencies and survival—rent, food, utilities) Yellow dock, peppermint, dried orange peel, sassafras, grains of paradise, hot peppers, allspice

Seven-Herb General Healing Dolly: White sage, hyssop, rosemary, lavender, lemon verbena, basil and nine acorns. The acorns are strung on a red thread and tied around the dolly's waist. Each day for nine days an acorn is removed and given back to nature off the property of the sick person. On the tenth day, regardless of the health of the individual, the doll is decommissioned and scattered off the property. If the sickness is severe, make one dolly per month until the individual has returned to full health.

You can also make these dolls using beeswax. I have found that you can microwave beeswax a minute or less at a time. Be careful, however, as the wax can catch fire. You can also melt the wax in a double boiler (still a fire hazard, so take care). Melt the wax to just about liquid, then watch as it cools for the right time for easy manipulation. Do a few trial runs with the wax until you are familiar with its consistency and handling.

Working with Found Stones

There is something very sacred about walking in the woods or by the sea and finding stones that speak to you. They seem to whisper—beauty, perhaps, or serenity. Maybe you feel strength or a sense of personal power when you hold the stone. In Braucherei and Granny Magick, plain stones (nothing fancy) are used both in attraction and banishing magick, and are employed as talismans, amulets, and poppets. Poppet stones can be carried in the pocket, used in conjuring bags, placed on the altar, hidden in dark places to affect the environment, left in a graveyard or a sacred place where you wish to forge a connection—their uses are only inhibited by your mind.

Before painting my stones I baptize them in a ritual fire, asking that all negativity be removed. Many times I will call upon a particular fire god or goddess or ask for the assistance of the angels of fire. Sometimes I invoke the planetary spirits. My choice is

SMOOTH STONES FROM NATURE MAKE
MARVELOUS POPPETS AND SPIRIT DOLLS

determined by my intention. After the stones have cooled, I submerge them in blessed water for twenty-four hours or from dawn to dawn. After the twenty-four hours, I remove the stones, dry them off, and place them in a plain brown paper bag until I am ready to paint them.

Painting stones is a very easy craft as long as you have patience and good brushes. After all my supplies have been cleansed and blessed, I begin by painting three base coats of gesso on the stones; this allows the finished color to visually pop and also cuts down on the number of color coats you will need. During this process be careful not to scratch the gesso with your fingernails or other objects. To help speed the drying process, I use a heat gun on low setting. Just as with the clay, I often add magical oils and a bit of herbal powder to the colored acrylic paint before application. Depending upon the opacity of your paint, your stones may need up to seven or eight coats to achieve the color vibrancy you desire. Using a heat gun or a hair dryer on low can speed the process along. Once the base color coats are completely dry, I focus on my intent and let the stone "tell" me how it wants to be decorated. When I'm finished painting and the stone is completely dry, I use an acrylic sealer to protect the paint from scratches, moisture, and dirt. I've found that an indoor/outdoor varnish is best, which can be brushed or sprayed on the stone. I let the sealer dry for at least twenty-four hours before placing the stone in the birthing pot.

Sacred Motherstone

The Sacred Motherstone is a physical connection to the Divine Mother in whatever form you see her. It is a link, a pathway, a road, a way to access the divine feminine energy that is always at your fingertips. This wishing spirit doll is designed to fit in the palm, small enough so that if you need to hold it in public, no one will see what is in your hand. I've found that the best way to choose a Motherstone is to open your mind, connect with the Sacred Mother, and ask that in your daily travels the right stone finds its way to you. Once you've found just the right stone, you will need gesso, paint brushes, paint, and acrylic sealer for decorating, and the following:

- 7 herbs that represent the Divine Mother to you (keep in mind that these herbs will be steeped in hot water, then left to cool overnight)

- 7 candles in color(s) that represent the Divine Mother to you (the size of the candles and their holders is up to you)

- your visualization of the Divine Mother (can be a picture, object, or just in your mind)

- an ice cube tray

- heatproof measuring cup (4-cup size)

- 4 cups spring water or water from a clean running spring or river (you can also use seawater)

- pot to warm the water on the stove

- wooden spoon

- glass bowl

- 1 ounce of vodka (optional)—this is a "spirit" linked metaphorically to both water and fire, and it is clear (therefore pure)

- find or write your own goddess chant that speaks to your heart

- double-check to make sure the varnish (sealer) that will be painted on the stone is waterproof (this is a necessity for this ceremony)

- magickal oil (optional) to dress the candles (rub a bit of oil on each candle)

The Motherstone has her own birthing process, different from those already provided. Before beginning, consider your magickal timing—what moon quarter speaks to you of the Divine Mother? What planetary energies do you associate with her? It takes three days to make your Motherstone. Once this choice is made, you are ready to create your Motherstone.

Cleanse and bless all supplies. On the first day, you will make the Motherstone elixir. On the second day, you will paint the stone. On the third day, you will empower your finished work.

On the first day, place your herb mixture in the heatproof measuring cup. Heat the water in a separate container. When it is just about to boil, remove the water from the heat and pour over the herb mixture. Stir the water/herb mixture slowly with the wooden spoon in the direction that you feel is most natural. During the stirring process, you can sing, chant, or listen to music. Allow yourself to connect with the Divine Mother, breathing deeply and blowing softly over the water as you stir. You might like to intone: "Gracious Mother, come to me."

When you feel calm, serene, and filled with love, stop stirring and drop the unpainted stone into the water. Let the stone sit in the water overnight. At dawn remove the stone from the water and dry it off. Pour the cooled herbal water into the ice cube tray. If there is any water left over, save it. Place the ice cube tray filled with the herbal water in the freezer. Take the leftover water and put it in a clean container. Store in the refrigerator. You can use it in other magickal applications as holy water.

Paint your Motherstone in any colors you desire, using the information under the Working with Found Stones section given earlier. Before you seal the stone with waterproof varnish, blow over the mouth of the stone three times, saying softly: "Sacred Mother, come to me." Seal the stone and allow it to dry overnight.

On the third day, when you are ready to empower the stone, place the glass bowl in the center of your altar. Fill the bowl with the herbal ice cubes. Hold the vodka up to your visualization of the Mother and ritually pour the vodka over the ice. Place the Motherstone on top of the vodka-soaked ice cubes. Surround the bowl with the seven candles. Breathe deeply three times.

Begin intoning the goddess chant that speaks to your heart. You could also play music that you feel is inspirational and helps you connect with the Divine Mother. Dress the candles, one by one. As you place each candle in its holder, say: "The Mother will appear."

When all the candles are dressed and placed back in their holders, working from left to right around the circle (counterclockwise), begin lighting each candle. As you light each candle, whisper: "The Mother is here!"

When you have lit the last candle, stand back and take several deep breaths, running energy from the ground up through your body to the top of your head, and as you exhale, continuing to run the energy into your heart chakra and out your hands, palms pointed toward the candles.

The next part of the ritual can either be spoken in your own words or you can say:

> *Sacred Mother, I call thee here to instill my life with happiness, health, joy, and harmony. Please fill this wishing stone made in your image with your divine power, so that I may connect my field with that of your own. Henceforth, whenever I hold this stone I will be strong. Whenever I hold this stone I will be confident. Whenever I hold this stone I will be courageous. Whenever I hold this stone I will be able to accomplish any task with ease and joy. Whenever I hold this stone I know that what I will and what I wish will come to pass, for thou art the Queen of Magick and the Divine Mother of all! Hail to thee, O Great Mother! As this ice melts and this fire burns, I command that this image absorbs your power and will henceforth be a conduit from thee to me!*

This conjuration can be used in other magick and enchantments—simply adjust the words according to what you are holding in your hands (a doll, a gemstone of a particular type, a rune, a photograph, etc.). It is an excellent empowerment for lucky pieces and gambling pursuits.

Dot the stone image with a tiny amount of magickal oil, then draw three equal-armed crosses in the air over the image to seal the work. Say:

As above, so below; this deed is done! Only the good remains!

Slap your hand (hard) on the altar.

Allow the candles to burn down and the ice to melt. When the candles are fully extinguished and the ice has completely melted, lift the image from the water and say:

By the power of the Divine Mother,
I raise thee in the name of the seven angels.
I raise thee in the name of the seven stars.
I raise thee in the name of the seven planets.
I raise thee in the name of the seven winds.
Thou art birthed to this physical world.
I command thee, energy, do my bidding—
I know thee will do this for me!

The rite is completed. Wrap your sacred Motherstone in a cloth that matches its color. Carry it with you to remind you of your connection to the Divine Mother.

To activate your Motherstone at any time, you can create your own chant or charm to be said as you softly rub the stone or you can simply memorize the chant given below, which is similar to the birthing chant. As you hold and rub the stone, state your desire—for example: "I wish for protection as I drive through the snowstorm today." If possible, let your breath flow over the stone as you speak.

By the power of the Divine Mother,
I awaken thee in the name of the seven angels.
I awaken thee in the name of the seven stars.
I awaken thee in the name of the seven planets.
I awaken thee in the name of the seven winds.
O Great Goddess, I connect my field with thine.
My desire is birthed into this physical world
And I receive the positive benefits—
I know thee will do this for me!

The Spirit Walk Poppet

Not everyone has tons of crafty stuff on hand. Not everyone feels the need to go shopping for artful embellishments. Not everyone wants to spend hours creating a poppet. Not everyone has special herbs or oils to enhance their work. Does that mean you can't make a poppet? Not at all! Some of the most powerful poppets can be made from items found around the house or from nature. Let's say that your sister called and your nephew is sick. She's taken him to the doctor, but she's still worried. "Can you do something right away?" she asks. Of course you can! Just set in your mind who the poppet is for (your nephew) and what you want to accomplish (healing). Then, speaking aloud, ask Spirit, the universe, a particular deity or angel by name, or a beloved ancestor to help you find what you need to make a poppet so Jeremy (let's call him that) will get better quickly.

You could also make a poppet that represents Jeremy's sickness. Your call—just be clear when you make your request. Take three deep breaths, relax, focus, and begin to walk around your living area or outdoors. Let intuition be your guide on your materials. In this example, I picked up a clothespin from the laundry room, a pipe cleaner from a drawer in the kitchen, moss from outside an old flower arrangement, electrical tape from the shed, and an indelible marker from the desk in the office. I cleansed and blessed all my supplies, then quickly put the poppet together. I only needed glue to stick the moss on the head of the clothespin. With the indelible marker, I can draw runes or other magickal sigils on the clothespin, or I can

write "Jeremy be well" on the poppet. Since I found a clothespin, I could even write a petition on a piece of paper and insert it into the slit. Next, I could use the Fast Track birthing method from chapter 4, which doesn't require any tools. To lend more power to my request, I might rummage in the kitchen cabinet, where I can find several cleansing/banishing herbs—rosemary, sage, thyme, and clove. I could cleanse, bless, and empower these herbs, then pop them in a plastic bag right along with Jeremy's poppet, or I could lay the poppet on a bed of the herbs in a glass bowl and then use the sending rite in chapter 4 to activate the poppet.

"Get Better" Rag Poppet
pattern on page 228

There are so many wonderful cotton colors and prints that I designed a rag poppet using the female poppet pattern. This style of doll uses machine stitching on the right sides of the doll (the doll isn't turned), leaving ragged edges. Once all the seams are clipped at ¼ inch (like a rag quilt), the doll is stuffed and washed, which creates the unique fraying. Soft and cuddly, this doll is perfect for empowering a child or for healing, and it can be made from pieces of clothing worn by the person that the poppet is for, cut into 2½-inch strips. Only work with used clothing if the doll is intended for the individual who has worn the clothing. For example, if you wanted to banish Aunt Amy's cancer, you wouldn't use your husband's old flannel shirt because his energy, not Aunt Amy's, is imbued into the clothing. If you don't have any clothing worn by the individual the doll is intended for, use new, freshly laundered quilting cotton for best results. The "Get Better" rag poppet is the perfect vehicle for giving positive energy.

Supplies Needed
- poppet pattern (the female gingerbread is a good choice)
- strips of 2½-inch-wide cotton approximately 16 inches long
- sewing machine (or you can hand stitch, which will take some time, or you could use Stitch Witchery strips)
- sharp scissors (I use a rotary cutter for the strips)
- pins

A FINISHED "GET BETTER" RAG POPPET

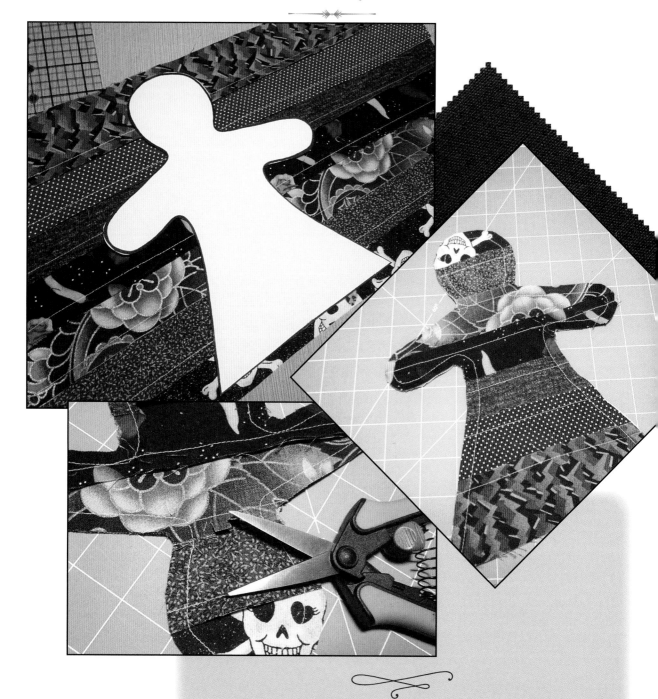

(CLOCKWISE FROM TOP LEFT) LAY THE POPPET PATTERN
ON THE SEWN STRIPS; THE POPPET AFTER BEING SEWED;
AND CLIPPING THE SEAMS BEFORE STUFFING

To make the doll, begin by cutting out the poppet pattern from your paper. Then cut enough 2½-inch-wide by 16-inch-long cloth strips to accommodate the size of the pattern plus about 1 inch. Lay the strips out to doublecheck sizing and color choices. I used seven strips for the female gingerbread pattern. Take two 16-inch-long strips and pin the wrong sides of fabric together (you will be sewing on the right side of the fabric). Using a ¼-inch seam, sew strips together. Continue adding strips one at a time, remembering to sew wrong sides together. Your seams will be on the outside of the finished doll.

Press all seams in one direction. Lay pattern on sewn strips to make sure you have pieced enough strips together. Fold sewn strips wrong sides together (so that you will have two poppet pieces that will match after cutting) and pin pattern to doubled fabric. Cut out poppet or use white chalk to outline the pattern directly on the strips, then sew along the white line. Finish by cutting out the doll using a ¼-inch seam allowance.

If you are going to add eyes (such as buttons or doll eyes with clip backs), consider affixing them before you sew the poppet together. Using a ¼-inch seam, sew poppet pieces (wrong sides together), leaving an edge open for stuffing. Since I loosely stuff this type of poppet, I left the entire bottom edge of the skirt open. After stuffing, it will be easy to close up with the sewing machine.

Before stuffing, I clip all seams except for the open bottom of the doll. This includes all the seams across the doll, front and back, and all the side seams. Leave about ⅛ inch or ¼ inch between clips, being careful not to cut your stitching.

Rag projects are meant to be washed—washing helps to create the ragged edges—so consider carefully what you will include in the poppet; polyfill or natural cotton is a good choice. If you want to add a petition, you can use indelible ink pen on pretreated muslin, then insert the piece of cloth into the doll with your chosen stuffing, or print a design on specially prepared muslin or canvas with your computer printer. You can usually find this product at a craft or sewing store. Once you have stuffed the poppet, sew the opening shut. Wash the poppet in cold water on a gentle cycle. Depending upon the type of stuffing you used, this poppet can also be placed in the dryer on a cooler setting.

If you want to put items in the doll that can't be run through the machine, wash and dry the doll body before stuffing. As the cotton may be all jumbled, press lightly with a steam iron, stuff the doll, add your special charms or herbals, and then sew up the doll.

The Goddess Poppet
pattern on page 234

The Goddess pattern is designed specifically for paper or felt construction (where the fabric is not turned after sewing). However, if you do make the doll with fabric, once she is turned, you can fold in the edges of the arms and hand stitch. After stitching, the hands will naturally draw together. However, they are still separated. If you wish to have the continuous circle of the arms, stitch the finished edges together.

If you would like the neck and body to be a bit firmer, you can insert a stabilizer into the doll's neck and body before stuffing. I used half a clothespin; you could also use pipe cleaners, a small natural stick, or a trimmed bamboo skewer (with sharp point filed off).

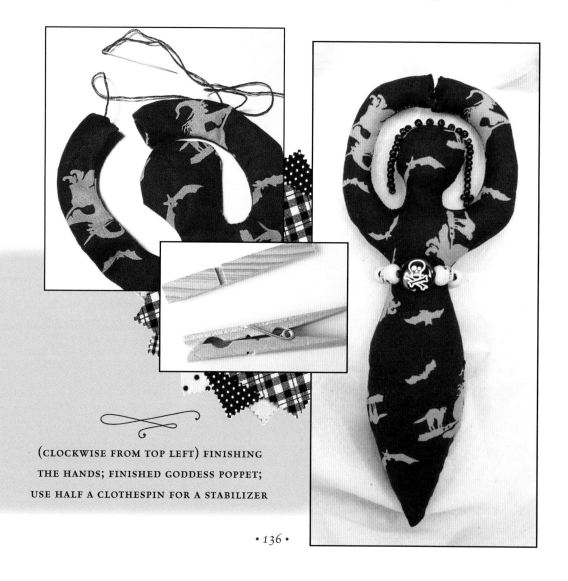

(CLOCKWISE FROM TOP LEFT) FINISHING
THE HANDS; FINISHED GODDESS POPPET;
USE HALF A CLOTHESPIN FOR A STABILIZER

Paper Poppets
pattern on page 228

You may not always have the time or the inclination to sit down and sew or glue a poppet together. The poppet patterns in this book can easily be used for paper; the rules of magick are the same. You can name, birth, and write your intent directly on the poppet. You can use colored pencils, crayons, markers, glitter, etc., to add your own special touch or you can use a computer program to turn your paper poppet into a work of digital art. When you are finished, roll up the poppet just as the ancient Greeks did and either tie it with thread or string or put a pin or nail through it. Your magick may be completed at that point, or you might like to use your paper poppet in a full ceremony or as a spell component in a conjuring bag.

The paper poppet on this page is the TrotterHead Paper Poppet, used to banish illness, evil people, ghosts, haints, and negativity. The image is that of the Angel of Scorpio. Notice that within the image there is a picture of the Helm of Awe to protect the practitioner. The head of the poppet is where you write the Braucherei conjuration for removing evil, which is given below; just keep writing over the top of the text, like a tangle. Use the black line on the poppet to write the name of the individual or thing you wish to remove from your life.

Write the following on the paper poppet:

> Trotterhead, I forbid thee in my home,
> I forbid thee in my place of employment,
> I forbid thee my prosperity,
> I forbid thee my job,
> I forbid thee my children and my spouse.
> Thou shalt be banished, and thee must count
> all the stars in the sky, all the hills on the earth,
> all the fish in the sea, and all the birds in the air.
> No peace, no rest, no sleep for thee.
> Thou art banished forever from me!

Vegetable and Fruit Poppets

Poppets can be made out of potatoes, onions, carrots, or other vegetables and fruits. Because they are organic and will rot, they are a perfect banishing vehicle. The vegetable or fruit can be left whole and decorated with an indelible marker or be cut in half, gouged, stuffed with herbs and sigils, wrapped with string to put the halves back together, and then buried in the ground. "As this potato rots, so shall the lies told by Jennifer rot in her mouth, and she shall be exposed!"—or—"As this potato rots and becomes one with the earth, so shall sickness and disease leave thee forever!"

Trees and other plants can be petitioned to assist you in your magick. For example, a stuffed potato poppet can be left inside a briar patch if your aim is to catch a criminal or trip up a liar. Leave the potato in the woods in the hour of Saturn (to capture and hold the evil person). Leave an offering to the plant or tree as a thank-you for assistance.

For good fortune, love, happiness, joy—all the energies of blessing—you can create the vegetable/fruit poppet with all edible components, bake or mix with the family's food, and distribute it among the dishes or place the dismembered poppet in just one recipe. You could also make a healthy treat, such as the applesauce poppet below. Apples are associated in magick with love, abundance, and good fortune.

Applesauce Love Poppet

Core and peel twenty-one certified organic apples. Cut into small cubes. Put into a pot with about one cup of water. Cook apples until they are tender and begin to fall apart. Remove from heat and drain if necessary. Mash cooked apples with fork or potato masher. Cool to room temperature.

Spray the inside of a cookie cutter with a small amount of olive oil. Put cookie cutter on a piece of parchment paper on a small plate. Pour some of the applesauce into the mold. Whisper love and joy over it, then pop it into the freezer.

After the remaining applesauce has cooled, place in a storage container in the refrigerator. When the poppet is completely frozen, take it out of the freezer and "send it" as you blend the poppet in with the remainder of the applesauce that you stored in the refrigerator. Alternatively, you can use the frozen poppet as an added ingredient in another dish you bake later on. If you plan to keep the frozen poppets for a while, slip them into a plastic freezer bag or container to keep them from freezer burn. This is a perfect love poppet because it can be ingested safely.

This recipe has no additives except your magick; therefore, the applesauce poppet formula can also be added as an ingredient for safe dog treats. For people, please note that you can add a small amount of sugar or cinnamon to this recipe.

Egg Poppets

Poppets made from eggs are useful for enchantments centering on birth, growth, and good fortune. They can also be used to take off illness and negative energy from one's body. You may be familiar with the European practice of running an uncooked egg (still in its shell) over the human body to remove sickness. The egg is "cast off," far away from the patient, usually with a statement of emphatic banishment. Some practitioners break the egg in the bowl to see if there is blood in it. If blood is there, the curse or illness continues, and more will have to be done. Unfortunately, the blood indicator doesn't work for commercially sold supermarket chain store eggs.

The Need Dolly

The need dolly is a figure crafted by yourself out of natural objects and imbued with power by your spoken word to draw to you what you need most. The image gathers your thoughts, ideas, experiences, and feelings for a given period of time (in this example, seven days). On the eighth day the practitioner releases the doll through one of the four elements, commanding the image to bring perfect solutions to the owner or other necessities that were vocally whispered over the doll during its creation. The need dolly can be used for a variety of desires, from bringing more food into the home to accomplishing a goal to banishing a long-term block. Once constructed, the need dolly should stay with you as much as possible so that it can "see" and experience your life. The more information it has about you, the better.

In 2017 I ran a week-long magickal release program on my Word Press blog (http://www.silverravenwolf.wordpress.com). When I implement these free offerings, I usually choose one unusual type of magickal application for the participants to try. For the January session we all made need dollies. Those utilizing the program were instructed to take a Spirit Walk and collect natural items to make their need dolly. Before the participants left home, they were advised to face the open front door and indicate the purpose of the Spirit Walk. They were also to ask for protection throughout their journey because sometimes we are so focused on the spirituality of something, we forget that the real world contains dangers we should avoid—stumbling in the woods and breaking an ankle would not be good. When they returned home, they were to construct their dolly in sacred space or a ritual circle—the choice was entirely theirs. Likewise, how the doll was constructed was also their choice. Some used twine, some glue, and others worked with yarn or wire, etc. The point is not an art masterpiece but a vehicle for intense magick that you have constructed yourself.

The success of the need dolly with these students was remarkable. They loved the dolls they made, and some took to calling the dolls their "needy dolly." I cautioned them early on *not* to become too attached to the spirit doll—that to keep in mind at all times that the doll would be released and not kept. Only in its release could it perform its ultimate job: that of bringing to you what you most need or want.

THIS NEED DOLLY WAS MADE FROM
ITEMS COLLECTED FROM THE WOODS

Once the doll is constructed, you whisper or speak to it as much as possible, telling it what you feel you really need in your life. You can create the doll with the main goal already in mind or you can use the doll as solution oriented wherein the image becomes a sounding board, allowing your own mind to consider, contemplate, and eventually choose the path you wish. Either choice works. Some of the practitioners burned a candle each day beside the dolly as an affirmation/offering (depends on the mindset of the student) toward their goal. Some painted their dolls with specific fluid condensers to ramp up the power (see my book *The Witching Hour* for a complete discussion on how to make fluid condensers).

On the eighth day the dolly is "sent" into the universe to bring back what is desired (your goal) by the use of one of the four elements—earth, air, water, fire (or a combination of elements). The doll can be deconstructed—or not; again, this is a choice the magickal worker must make, and it relies a great deal on one's belief system or set of limits one has imposed on one's world. I know that sounds snooty, but that is really how it is. Your magick is boosted or hindered by yourself, your actions, and your own thoughts. Bottom line: your dolly can do anything you want it to—however, you have to believe that what you ask is possible. Where some try to micromanage the magick, others simply say "I don't care how you do it, just get it done as long as you don't hurt anyone" when they are commanding the dolly.

It can take from only a few hours up to thirty days for your need dolly to manifest your command. The timing depends upon a number of factors:

- Your mindset. Were you confident? Is this what you really wanted? Is your subconscious in tune with your conscious desires?

- What needs to change within yourself to receive your desire.

- What needs to change outside of yourself to receive your desire.

- Where have you placed the power for your life? With someone else? With yourself?

There are occasions when you think something is very simple—yet, in the universal pathworking of energy, it is difficult, and many alignments are necessary. Conversely, there are instances where you think your desire is incredibly difficult, but it isn't at all! You have needlessly complicated the process with the machinations of your brain. If you always try to do the right thing and your confidence in yourself is stable, your need dolly should work just fine.

——»✦«——

Cookie-Cutter Poppets

Metal and plastic cookie cutters shaped like humans or animals are fun and easy to work with in magick. These types of dolls usually fall into the disposable category; however, you also can use them for amazing permanent polymer clay creations that you can turn into jewelry, ritual tool decorations, or other crafty ideas. For the Kitchen Witch, making enchanted cookies is an old trick, and it's so much fun with the cookie-cutter image! Cookies made with ginger and cinnamon can be enchanted to bring self-empowerment, health, good fortune, etc. Below are ideas for disposable poppets using cookie cutters in unique and crafty ways.

Loose Herb Poppet—Air & Earth Magick

You will need a cookie cutter of any size in the shape of a male or female human or an animal, a small piece of paper, a pen or pencil, and a selection of loose herbs that match your purpose. The herbs can be dressed with magical oils, powders, or fluid condensers that match your intent. Write your desire on the paper and then burn the paper. When the ashes are cool, add them to the loose herb mixture.

Outside, in a magick circle or sacred space, pour a glass of blessed water on the ground. Allow the water to seep into the dirt. Next, set the cookie cutter directly on the wet ground. Pour the herb mixture into the cookie cutter. Do not remove the cookie cutter just yet.

Light a match, blow the smoke across the image, then put the match out in the herbal mix. Add the match to the doll. Place one hand on either side of the herb-filled image. Blow your breath softly across the image, saying:

> With breath of three you come alive.
> With breath of three you come alive.
> With breath of three you are alive!
> Live! Live! Live!

Infuse your intent into the doll with visualization and words. All this time, your hands should still be in contact with the earth. Finally, command the doll to fulfill your desire. Seal the working by drawing an equal-armed cross in the air over the surface of the herbal mix. Remove the cookie cutter. Take up the energy of the circle and direct it into the doll. Turn and walk away. The element of air will do the rest.

Bird Seed Love and Good Fortune Spirit Doll

Why not spend a few hours—or several hours over the course of a weekend—to make something edible for wild birds? Focusing on animals and their needs can bring that feeling of worth that is necessary for balanced happiness. It shifts our emotional state to the beauty of the earth and her gifts, and it builds unconditional love energy around us. As you create your birdseed delights, daily cares and worries slip away. Gifting the birds your treats at dawn can bring a whole new meaning to the intermingling of human and nature—you just have to allow the happiness to encompass you! As the birds eat your poppet, your desire breaks free of the image form and births into the universe. This type of poppet, to me, is one of the most fulfilling, as it meets the needs of human and animal at the same time.

When offering your poppet to the birds, you may wish to choose a god or goddess energy tuned to air or our feathered friends. Goddesses associated with birds include Rhiannon (Celtic), Isis (Egyptian), Nekhbet Vulture Goddess (Egyptian—hers was the largest cult within the City of the Dead), Hecate (Greek—she shapeshifts into an owl, as do Celtic goddesses Blodeuwedd and Arianrhod), the Morrighan (Celtic—crow/raven), etc. You may wish to spend some time doing a search on the internet for bird mythology as it relates to both male and female deities. Many shamans in a number of cultures thought that birds gifted them with second sight. Birds are often associated with creation myths, the element of air, and the ability to speak with spirits.

This formula is generous in ingredients. I used a large cookie cutter shaped like a female. Use a whisper magick chant such as:

For Love: "As surely as the birds and animals consume this cake, so love and joy will be my fate."

For Money: "As surely as the birds and animals consume this cake, so good fortune and prosperity will be my fate!"

I whispered this second chant as I prepared the poppet cake, and then again before I took the finished poppet outside to give to nature. For good fortune, make the poppet on a Thursday (Jupiter Day) or a Sunday in the planetary hour of Venus, the sun, or Jupiter (depending upon the nature of the good fortune you desire) when the moon is waxing. For love, I would choose Friday (Venus Day) in the planetary hour of Venus when the moon is waxing.

I found the larger cookie cutters to work better than the smaller ones. If you only desire to make one poppet, put what is left of your ingredients into silicon molds sprayed with nonstick cooking spray. You can share these cakes with the birds whenever you like for a variety of other magickal activities. They are an excellent offering to the gods and goddesses of birds/air/animals during formal ritual.

The following collection of ingredients will make more than one poppet.

DELUXE BIRDSEED POPPET RECIPE
3 cups birdseed

3 tablespoons corn syrup or molasses

3 tablespoons chunky peanut butter

1 handful raisins

¾ cup stoneground cornmeal

½ cup boiling water

1 packet unflavored gelatin

Cookie cutter or silicon mold

Nonstick cooking spray

Straws cut into 3-inch lengths—use these to make holes so that you can decorate and hang your poppet

Wax paper

THE MAGICK

Pour the cornmeal onto a flat surface covered with the wax paper. Draw sigils, initials, or words in the cornmeal that represent your desire. Seal this image by drawing an equal-armed cross in the air over the cornmeal. Put the cornmeal back with your other supplies until you are ready to make the poppet. As you make the poppet, intone your favorite chant or one of the whisper chants given above.

MAKING THE BIRDSEED COOKIE CUTTER IMAGE

In a large bowl mix the birdseed, corn syrup, peanut butter, raisins, and cornmeal. Mix well; use your hands if you have to so that the peanut butter and syrup are spread throughout the birdseed. Spray the inside of your cookie cutter or mold with the nonstick cooking spray. Put the cookie cutter or mold on the wax paper on a level surface that can be transported to the refrigerator.

Boil the water and slowly stir gelatin into the water. When gelatin powder is completely dissolved, pour the warm liquid over the birdseed mixture. Mix thoroughly. Quickly spoon warm mixture into the cookie cutter or mold. Pack as tightly as you can. I use a flat wooden spatula to really press the seed into the mold. If you desire, place one straw in the center of each poppet or cake. Push it all the way to the bottom. This will make a hole for hanging the poppet when it has finished drying. Placing the straw in the center keeps the string or ribbon from tearing through the doll or cake right away. If you are using a cookie cutter (not a mold), you can carefully slide the cookie cutter up and off of the image, or you can pop the whole thing into the refrigerator and remove the cookie cutter later. No matter your choice, refrigerate the poppet for at least 2 hours.

Carefully remove the poppet from the refrigerator, checking to make sure it is fairly firm—it will still be delicate and can crumble easily. If you are in a hurry and the poppet has not fallen apart, you can use it immediately in magick (such as further spell work or ritual) and then give it to the birds. However, if you want your poppet to be more stable and not so squishy—let the poppet air dry for 48 hours or place it in a food dehydrator for 7 hours at 115 degrees. My poppet was 1.5 inches thick—if your poppet is thinner, it will need less time in the food dehydrator.

Add ribbon or twine if you wish to hang the poppet as a decoration—or you can simply crumble the image after the magick is completed and put the pieces in a flat pan birdfeeder.

Here is an alternate version using the same instructions but fewer ingredients.

Simple Birdseed Poppet Recipe

   3 cups birdseed

   1 cup boiling water

   2 packages gelatin

   1 teaspoon finely ground eggshell (used as grit for birds)

   Nonstick cooking spray

   Cookie cutter or silicon mold

   Wax paper

Draw your sigils, words, or images in the finely ground eggshell.

Hounds of Hel Dog Treat Poppet

Ghostly packs of dogs pepper our magickal history and are incredibly useful in certain enchantment applications, including protection and banishment of unwanted energies. They can even be used if you feel you are being haunted by attentions of the unwanted dead—use vinegar to dispel the dead and place the dog treats in a triangle outside of the magickal circle for Cerberus, commanding him to take the offending ghost back across the River Styx to the land of the dead! Whether we desire to attune with the energies of Odin's war hounds, Cerberus (Greek three-headed hound that guarded the entrance to Hades), the visage of the Egyptian Anubis, Herne the Hunter's nighttime gallop, the Wild Huntsman of Dartmoor with yell hounds, Greek goddess Hecate's faithful guardian hounds, the Nordic goddess Hel and her hellhound Garmr, Cwn Annwn, the Welsh spectral hounds of Annwn, or a multitude of other legends, you may find these safe, organic dog treats perfect for your familiar in this world or for honoring the canines of the ghostly otherworld realms. You can shape these treats into images of people or animals, and they are okay to set out in the wild as offerings in the woods. Given your imagination, there really is no end to their use!

INGREDIENTS

2½ cups garbanzo bean organic flour

2 eggs from free-range chickens

¾ cup organic pumpkin

¼ cup water or antibiotic-free chicken
  or beef stock that you make yourself—
  be sure there are no onions in your stock

Preheat oven to 350 degrees F (175 degrees C). Whisk together the flour, eggs, and pumpkin in a bowl. Use the chicken/beef stock to make the dough workable, adding a little at a time (you most likely won't use it all). Using brown rice flour or the garbanzo bean flour, spread a little flour on your working surface and on the dough if necessary to make the consistency workable. Roll the dough flat to ½ inch with a nonstick rolling pin. Use cookie cutters to cut out shapes in the dough (human or animal images). You could also roll the dough into a log, then cut the log into ½-inch pieces. Bless the treats before they go into the oven. If you know your purpose, instill that energy into the dough as well. Bake until hard, about 40 minutes. Allow to cool. They will keep in the refrigerator about 2 weeks; 6 months if you freeze them.

Please note that other ingredients can be added to this mixture; however, I purposefully made this formula super safe—no GMO additives, no salt, no sugar, no wheat, no corn, no gluten, no preservatives, etc. This is as basic and safe as it gets with current research.

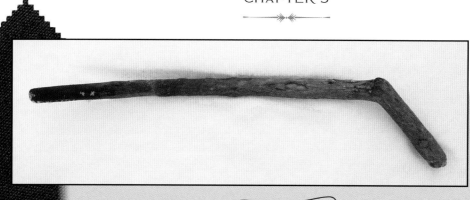

IN WHISPER MAGICK A STICK SCORCHED IN RITUAL FIRE
IS USED TO "WITNESS" A MAGICKAL WORKING. THIS
WITNESS STICK ALSO CAN BE EMPLOYED TO DRAW DESIGNS
IN DIRT, SNOW, MUD, OR WATER. SOMETIMES THE STICK
IS KEPT AND USED REPEATEDLY; ON OTHER OCCASIONS IT
IS USED ONLY ONCE, AND WHEN THE DESIRED OUTCOME
HAS COME TO PASS, THE STICK IS DESTROYED.

Mud Poppet

The mud poppet for sacred release or sacred birth is made of dirt or clay mixed with dirt, preferably from your local area, as you are in tune with the earth energies there. The dirt can also come from a sacred place in the woods or a graveyard (preferably from an ancestor's grave who was a decent person). The easiest way to create an image is to mix dirt, the ashes of the person's name (you can write the individual's name on a piece of paper or you can write the person's name three times on the back of their photo and burn in a fire-safe dish), and water in a bowl. Spray the cookie cutter with cooking spray or brush the cutter thoroughly on the inside with your favorite magickal oil. Magickal powders that match your intent can be added to the dirt/water mix, as well as a liquid fluid condenser if you so desire.

Once infused with the intent and given the command on the completion of the task, the doll either can be crumbled and buried in the ground (at least a foot deep for banishing activities) or placed on a mound with a cooked egg on its stomach. Animals will remove the egg (the birth of the thing), and rainwater will eventually dissolve the doll.

Beeswax Sandwich Cauldron Poppet/Spirit Doll

I originally designed this type of poppet to be burned in a cauldron. Simply cut out two poppets from a flat beeswax sheet with your cookie cutter. Use the cookie cutter to trace the third image on a piece of paper, leaving an extra inch of paper at the bottom of each foot of the image. Write your intent on the paper. Dress the paper with magickal oil, perfume, or liquid fluid condenser (remember that all three options can be flammable, depending upon the ingredients). Sandwich the paper between the two wax pieces, making sure that there is about an inch of paper exposed at the bottom of each foot. Empower the poppet. To activate the poppet, light the exposed paper pieces and blow across the poppet several times to feed the flame. Drop the poppet into the cauldron. Send the poppet as it burns. You can also use a ritual outdoor bonfire, throwing the poppet into the fire and sending as the flames rise.

Snow Poppet

Write your intent on a piece of paper with ink that will bleed. Outside, put the paper on a portable, flat surface such as your candleboard. Spread the snow on top of the paper. Use a cookie cutter to make the human image out of the snow (or if the snow is the right consistency, you can simply mold your own doll). Birth and command the doll. In most climates, the temperatures will not allow a snow poppet to live very long. Use the melting process as an integral part of your magick. You can leave the poppet outside or bring the snow spirit doll inside for an immediate ritual. You could even put your snow poppet in the freezer, if necessary; for example, put the Isa rune on its chest to stop or slow down a particular energy. Don't forget, you can use the traditional snowman, complete with carrot nose and coal or wooden button (no plastic) eyes, as a magnificent giant poppet! As he melts, so an avalanche of good fortune and happiness will flood your property, your home, and your life!

Salt Dollies
patterns on pages 240 & 241

In magick, salt is the universal cleanser. No matter what you wish to banish, send away, diminish, or destroy, salt is normally a primary ingredient. I have created two types of salt dollies that I use in workings to protect or heal people in my whisper magick/ Braucherei workings that can provide a powerful influence in your healing work.

Salt Dolly-Do to Banish Sickness and Nightmares

Salt Dolly-Do is to banish nightmares, sickness, and instability in the individual's life. Salt Dolly-Do is placed in your bed for seven nights. If you have pets, you may wish to put her in your pillow case behind your pillow to keep her from being tortured by your favorite feline or canine. Salt Dolly-Do has a pointed head and an open body cavity that is filled with salt, lavender, and rosemary, then sewn shut at the bottom of the skirt. The pointed hat/head can be folded over and pinned to a pillow.

Salt Dolly-Do is made of simple, inexpensive muslin because she is burned on the eighth day. I do not recommend using felt for this type of poppet because that material is usually difficult to burn. During the seven nights/days she sleeps with you, she is busy collecting all sickness and negativity that is surrounding you or in your aura. She can be dressed with additional magickal oils if you like—just make sure the oils don't bleed into your bedding. A favorite sigil or another item of healing can also be added to the doll if you desire.

You could also hang the image off the bedpost or place her on a shelf that is in the headboard or over the bed. Hang the doll from a suitable, temporary hook on the wall as close to the bed as possible. On the eighth day, take Salt Dolly-Do outside and burn her in a cauldron, intoning a suitable banishing chant such as:

> *Evil, begone; do not return!*
> *The horse has run off and the bridges are burned!*

Remember to thank Dolly-Do for her service to you and wish her well in her next incarnation. After the flames die down, seal the working by drawing an equal-armed cross in the air over the cauldron. When the ashes are cold, dump or bury them.

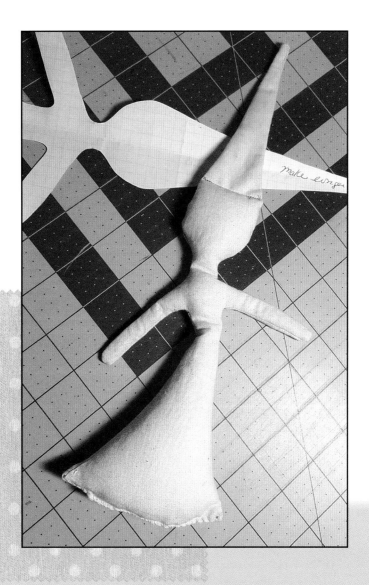

TO MAKE A SALT DOLLY-DO, SIMPLY ADJUST ONE
OF THE PATTERNS IN THIS BOOK BY ADDING
A **6**-INCH CONE HAT EXTENSION

Susie Salt Healer's Tool

I developed Susie Salt to be worn by Reiki, Braucherei, and Whisper Magick practitioners to protect them as they work with friends, family, and clients to remove illness or bring balance into their lives. Her head is elongated, and the opening to the doll is at the top of this head. Unlike Salt Dolly-Do, Susie Salt is not burned and can be used repeatedly—she is a permanent poppet and can be made from a variety of cotton materials. When completed, the doll is filled with salt, one piece of amethyst (or another gemstone), and lavender or other light, banishing dried herbs. Magickal sigils on paper can also be added.

The first Susie Salt dolls I made were completely filled with coarse blessed sea salt—however, this makes them rather heavy. I found that a salt herbal mixture is easier to handle, such as lavender, rosemary, lemon verbena, white sage (ground fine), and coarse sea salt. The top of Susie Salt is tied shut and is long enough to loop over your ritual cords or belt. That way, she hangs like a tool or decoration. She is your healing buddy and can be decorated by adding ribbons, jewels, bells, beads, etc., to make her completely unique. Her job is to remove all negativity coming toward you from other people. She is a defensive poppet. Because of the way I constructed her, she can be easily emptied, washed, dried, and filled many times again.

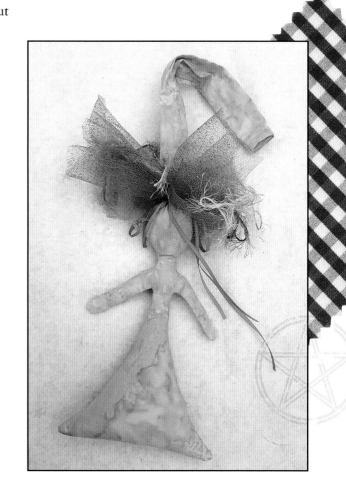

To make a Susie Salt doll, add a 2-inch by 11-inch extension to the head of one of the patterns in this book. When sewing, leave the top of the tube open. After turning the doll, you can fold the raw edges inward for a neater appearance. Fill the doll with a selection of salt and herbs. The more herbs, the lighter the doll.

Oppit Sandwich Dolls—Intent Dollies
patterns on pages 244 & 245

Oppit means "opportunity"! I designed these flat dolls for their easy portability. I call them sandwich dolls because they are a combination of layered fabric stabilizer and colorful material, not stuffed. The stiff design makes these spirit dolls easy to tuck in a purse, backpack, Book of Shadows, glove compartment of your car, etc. They also make the most unusual gift decoration on the outside of a wrapped box or basket. Oppits can be hung over your bed, added to wreaths on your door, wrapped around and glued to a jar—the ideas are endless! Oppit dolls are a great use for scrap cloth and even pieces from favored clothing that is no longer wearable but you would like to keep the material design and the connection to that person (if the clothing belonged to someone else). If you love quilting, use your pieced scraps to create a uniquely colorful doll with strips, blocks, and other pieced designs.

This type of doll goes together quickly with my unusual piecing method. Simply cut out three matching large squares—the fabric for the back of the doll, the stabilizer in the center, and the fabric for the front of the doll. Sandwich the squares together (right sides facing out). Lay your pattern directly on the square stack. Pin in the center so the pattern doesn't move. Beginning at the bottom, sew around the edges of the paper pattern. Stop when you are 2 inches from completion on the bottom. Tuck an empowered sigil in the opening. I use a bamboo skewer to push the paper into the doll as far as it will go. This is a substitute for the geist bag (see chapter 3). When you are satisfied with the positioning of the paper, stitch the remaining 2 inches. Take your time. Once you have sewn completely around the doll, remove the pattern. Use very sharp scissors to cut ¼ inch all the way around the outside edges.

You're done. If you are worried about fraying, you can use a no-fray product to treat the edges of the doll. Both stabilizer and the no-fray product are available at most fabric stores. The stabilizer is available in white and black. I prefer the black.

Add embellishments such as beads, sequins, and charms, then paint on the eyes with acrylic paint. Your Oppit is good to go!

I have provided two Oppit designs for you: the Sun Goddess Oppit (also called the Chakra Oppit) and the Witch Oppit. Oppits can be made of felt as well, using a glue gun or stitching, which would be a great project for your children!

Because they are flat and soft, Oppits work extremely well as Book of Shadows/personal journal protection dolls. Simply list her/his duties on a small piece of paper and slip inside the head before stitching. I usually spray my paper with universal fluid condenser and then dot with a bit of kyphi oil.

PAINTING THE EYES IS A
PROCESS OF CAREFULLY
LAYERING COLORS ON TOP
OF A BASIC WHITE SHAPE
THAT HAS BEEN OUTLINED IN
BLACK; THE MORE LAYERS, THE
BETTER THE EYES WILL POP.

Hermes Mercury Dreaming Doll
patterns on pages 227 & 236

The purpose of the dreaming doll is to provide a pathway for information or solutions to come to you in dreams, just like the doll used to help the queen mentioned at the beginning of this book. This doll uses the easy male poppet pattern, but you can use any pattern you desire. I have also added a pattern for a shirt and skirt, should you wish to make your poppet a bit more ephemeral. Unique dreaming charms can be added if you like, particularly if they are silver or have associations with Hermes or Mercury. What makes the doll special is the intent, the sigil provided, and the herb selection. I also made the doll a dreaming bed (just like in the story) filled with the same herbal formula. The doll can be placed on its pillow beside your bed or you can put the pillow under your own, allowing the fragrance of the herbs to help you in dreaming magick.

The herbal combination for the dreaming doll is a blend of lavender, mugwort, peppermint, marjoram, horehound, dill, and lemongrass.

The Hermes sigil (see following page) can be activated and placed within the doll, within its dream pillow/bed, or pinned on the outside of the doll. For my dreaming doll, I placed one sigil in the doll and one in the bed, with a general call for aid from Hermes. Then, when I need specific answers, I can pin a third sigil on the outside of the doll, writing my request on the sigil's blank side. I put the sigil in the doll and in the pillow so that if I wish, I can place the doll's bed under my pillow and use it as a sachet. You can leave the sigil as is and simply write your desire on the back of it, dress it with oil, and fold it like a sandwich to pin to the doll (so that you can use the doll again) or you can make the intent general and place the sigil on the inside of the doll. You can use the key given in the illustration to draw a sigil on the numbered box, putting a dot at each corresponding number and then drawing a line to connect the dots.

Timing

Possible construction and activation astrological timing would include new moon; full moon; moon in Pisces, Scorpio, Cancer, Gemini, or Aquarius; on a Wednesday or a Monday in the hour of the moon or Mercury; or at midnight. As a note, Mercury rules Gemini and Virgo.

To create your specialized sigil, write out your desire on a piece of paper. Using the key provided below, match the first letter of each word with its corresponding number. For example, "inspiration in my business" would create the number sequence 9942, factored to 942. Find the 9 in the square and draw a point. Next, find the 4 and draw a line from the 9 to the 4, then find the 2 and draw a line from the 4 to the 2, with a circle denoting the endpoint. Those lines are your sigil.

8	58	59	5	4	62	63	1
49	15	14	52	53	11	10	56
41	23	22	44	45	19	18	48
32	34	35	29	28	38	39	25
40	26	27	37	36	30	31	33
17	47	46	20	21	43	42	24
9	55	54	12	13	51	50	16
64	2	3	61	60	6	7	57

Hermes

KEY FOR DRAWING SIGILS FROM MAGICKAL SQUARES

1	2	3	4	5	6	7	8	9
A	B	C	D	E	F	G	H	I
J	K	L	M	N	O	P	Q	R
S	T	U	V	W	X	Y	Z	

To Make the Dreaming Doll Shirt and Skirt

Follow the pattern provided on page 236, cutting the shirt from a single piece of fabric and the skirt from a folded (doubled) piece of fabric (so that the skirt piece is wider due to the fold). The single pattern provided functions as the pattern for both the skirt and the shirt.

1. After you have cut both the skirt and the shirt, fold over one long side (as shown on the pattern) ¾ inch and press. Stitch a ½-inch seam to create the casing.

2. Attach a cord or ribbon to a safety pin and draw the cord or ribbon through the casing created by your stitching. Do this on both the shirt and skirt pieces. In measuring the cord or ribbon, double the length of the casing so you don't accidentally pull the ribbon or cord out of the casing.

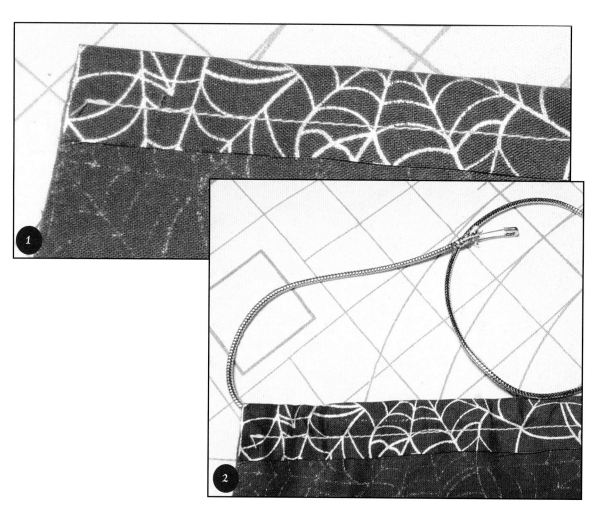

3. Once you have pulled the cord or ribbon through the casing on both the shirt and skirt, cut material in ¼- or ⅛-inch strips up to the seam line. Be careful not to cut into your stitching.

4. Gather material along cord or ribbon by pushing both sides of the casing to the center. Tie onto the doll. You can use this type of shirt/skirt for other projects or decorate other types of dolls, including a dried gourd doll, where the design becomes a unique collar around the neck of the gourd. Thread bells and beads onto the bottom of the fabric strips and tie.

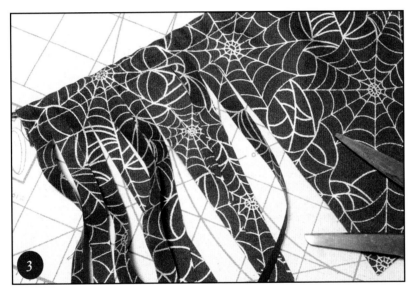

5. Add any embellishments to the clothing that you desire or simply knot the ends of the strips for a unique look.

6. The photo shows the dreaming doll lying on her dream pillow. Notice I chose a spiderweb pattern for both the doll's clothing and the dream pillow. This is to enhance the energy of capturing information in dreamtime. The blue glass is an oil lamp designed specifically for a mixture of olive oil blended with essential oils. Essential oils used in the example are lavender, lemongrass, peppermint, pine, and violet. The herbs and the sigil shown are those that are in the doll and the dream pillow.

7. The dreaming doll is birthed in the name of Hermes (Mercury), and each time she is activated, the power of Hermes is called upon to aid her in her mission. The photo shows the prepared dreaming doll with the sigil pinned to her chest. The dreaming lamp burns softly, filling the field of potential around the doll with a calm and peaceful aroma. Command the doll by whispering your request close to the head, making sure your breath flows across the doll's face. In this picture, the dreaming doll is ready to take her journey into dreamtime and bring her owner the requested information.

The spiderweb pattern I used in this doll enhances the energy of capturing information in dreamtime. Use your fabric prints to enhance your poppet magick!

Little Spirits

pattern on page 231

Little Spirits are great vehicles for a single focus or intent, such as love, money, etc. They don't take long to make and are wonderful gifts for children and adults alike. Think of them as an upgraded herbal sachet with eyeballs and a personality.

LITTLE SPIRITS PACK A LOT OF ENERGY PUNCH. SMALL ENOUGH TO CARRY IN PURSE OR POCKET, THEY CAN BE CREATED FOR GOOD LUCK, TO REMOVE A JINX, TO PROVIDE PROTECTION, OR TO PULL IN SUCCESS.

Grave Guardian for Ancestor Communication
pattern on page 233

This type of doll or spirit animal is made to connect you with your ancestors for honor, protection, and advice. The formula is thought to link the two worlds for easier communication. You can create the image several ways, celebrating the freedom to choose all aspects of the design and formula that mean the most to you. For example, you can gather grave dirt from one cemetery or from the graves of ancestors resting in several locations. You can choose those ancestors that you know a great deal about or go for the gusto and collect as many as you can. Your logic, your feelings, and your heart center can provide the answers that are right for you. A friend of mine didn't make an image at all. Instead, she purchased a skull bottle from a local liquor store and emptied the contents on the ground as an offering to the gods. She let the bottle completely dry and stuffed it with pictures, names, mementos, dried flowers, pennies, dried coffee (for the guardian of the crossroads), and the dirt from every locally buried ancestor. Before she entered each graveyard, she gave an offering of white rum and a cigar at the gates and carried a lit white candle on her journey to and from each grave.

My favorite herbs for a grave guardian (which can be any shape: human, animal, or otherwise) are patchouli, vetiver, sandalwood, peppermint, and coffee beans mixed in ritual with a few drops of cypress oil. I empower the doll with a burgundy candle dressed with a mixture of white rum and patchouli essential oil (be careful that you don't use too much rum or the candle could torch and cause a fire). Should you choose only one ancestor and you knew that person well, your choices of what goes into the doll might encompass the favorite aromas of the individual linked to small trinkets they once owned.

I always handle my grave guardians with respect. Prayers once a week on the day you desire should be given to the universe to bless the deceased. The grave guardian can also be buried at the gravesite to protect the dead, should you feel this is needed. Add juniper berries to the stuffing and a protective sigil if you wish to use the doll in this way.

In the photo on the next page, the grave guardian has beaded hair, which is very easy to do. The hair is usually one of the last embellishments I add to any doll. For most projects, I like glass E beads, a thin beading needle, and three strands of embroidery thread that match the color of the bead, although you can use special beading thread if you desire. I don't work with regular thread because the weight of the beads will eventually snap that type of thread, leaving you with a bald dolly and all that beading work scattered on the floor. Your bead choices are unending—don't be afraid to experiment! Use color, texture, and material that suit the project's energy.

To create the beaded hair, I put a knot at the end of the thread, then shoot the needle somewhere in the top center of the head. Depending upon the type of material you used, you can actually pop the knot through the material to the inside of the doll by tugging gently—just be careful you don't put the thread totally out of the doll. Once you hear the "snick" sound, stop. Thread as many E beads onto the combined three strands of embroidery thread to get the length of beads you feel matches the style of the doll. (They usually let you know, these dolls, if you listen.) Once you reach the desired length, add three more beads, then turn your needle and count up those three beads. Insert the needle in the fourth bead up from the bottom bead and pull gently. The last three beads will pull together in a cluster. Continue running the needle and thread back up through the strand, being careful not to miss any beads (or you will have an unsightly thread on the outside of one or more beads). When you reach the scalp, pull the thread tightly to remove any gaps in the string of beads. It is okay to run your fingers over the bead string to massage that thread taute inside the beads. Pull the thread again, then make a stitch in the head to secure the string of beads. You can run the needle back into the head and out at another spot to add another string of beads if your thread is long enough. If not, tie off and start over at a different place on the doll's head.

Grave guardians are usually most happy to travel with you in purse or pocket (depending upon the size), on long trips, to the job when you are having a bad time, etc. You may wish to make a special bag for the dolls, including some "food" for its travel; a few pieces of hard candy work well. If you need to link a place to yourself, suck on the hard candy for several minutes, close your eyes, think of creating the link, and then spit the candy on the ground. The link can "hold" for quite some time, regardless of what happens to the candy, depending upon your previous meditative and empowerment practice.

Gnome/House Spirit
pattern on page 243

Home protectors and household deities emanate from various cultural practices and colorful folklore all over the world. From the Slavic *domovoi* to the Anglo-Saxon brownie, gnomes and their like are associated with the earth element, good fortune, domestic bliss, and family protection. It is not uncommon to see a particular area set aside in a Pagan household focused on honoring the deities of the home itself. This focus includes the energy pattern of the structure coupled with nature that manifests in a design the owner acknowledges (often in the shape of a gnome, fairy, or mythical animal). These special places are limited only by the imagination and often cyclic offerings are shared. Fairy gardens and gnome houses are common, particularly around potted plants and terrariums. All my porch plants in the summer have a compendium of gnome/fairy/magickal animal activity, including a tiny barn and other unusual miniatures. Porch plants just seem so bare without such decorations, you know? And gnomes *love* little toys.

Should you wish to build your own village or family of gnomes, I have designed a fun, quick pattern out of felt for your enjoyment. These gnomes (fairies, trolls, or elves) can be filled with magickal gems and herbs and created with specific intent (love, money, good fortune, protection) or you can make them just because! These magickal beings can be any color, shape, or size. Feel free to adjust the pattern to make your little people more unique. Steps for completion are simple. All you need is a variety of felt, a good pair of sharp scissors, something for the nose (pom-pom, metal brad, wooden bead), polyester or cotton stuffing (which I used for inside the hat and some in the body to pack the herbs), a choice for hair (thick yarn or needle felting wool), and embellishments such as beads, sequins, or embroidery thread. You can use a glue gun or machine or hand stitch your gnomes. In my examples here, I used a combination of all three.

Begin by making any adjustments you would like to your pattern (a crooked hat or curled shoes, etc.). Cut out the paper pattern and then cut out your felt pieces. You do not need to add a seam allowance unless you want to. For my gnome, I cut one hat, two bodies, and four shoe pieces—one color for the top of the shoes and a different color for the bottom.

I've found that doing all embroidery additions before I assemble the gnome makes the project go easier and faster. However, if you will be machine stitching the hat or body, you will want to save the beadwork, charms, or sequins until after you have assembled the pieces because the pressure foot of the machine goes wonky around those objects.

PIECES OF GNOME

ADDING EMBELLISHMENTS

Sew the hat (right side to left side). I used the machine so I could turn the hat and hide the seam. I used a ¼-inch seam allowance and trimmed the seam before turning the hat.

Finish adding sequins and beads onto the hat. Stuff the top inch or inch and a half of the hat with poly-stuffing. This plumps out the hat. You can also add a small crystal or gemstone in the very top point of the hat for more magickal oomph.

Sew or glue three sides of the body together (two sides and top). I machine stitched the body so I could hide the seams. Trim the seams and turn the body inside-out so the seams don't show on the outside. If you don't want to use a machine, you can hand stitch or use a glue gun. Leave the bottom of the body open. Finish adding any beaded or sequin embellishments.

Stuff the body with your herb/gemstone blend that corresponds to the intent of the gnome. Pack the herbs into the body by adding the polyester or cotton stuffing last, leaving about ¼ to ½ inch unobstructed.

Decorate the top part of the shoes, then glue the tops of the shoes to the bottoms. Allow to cool (if you are using a glue gun). Once cool, arrange the shoes on the inside edge of the body (you want the shoes to stick out). Glue in place. When the shoes are secure, carefully glue the bottom edges of the body together. Take your time. Use a bamboo skewer to push the stuffing or any errant herbs into the body as you close it. You could also hand stitch the bottom closed if you prefer. (Oh, and as a note? Gnomes love unique shoes. Just saying…)

Cut 2 or 3 inches of thick yarn for mustache or beard. I twisted the fiber for a better hold in gluing. You can also use faux fur or felting wool. Remember that you can trim the hair and beard at the end of the project, rather than worrying about the length while you are putting all your pieces together.

Slip the hat down over the body as far as it naturally falls. There will be a little gap between the lower edge of the hat and the front/back of the body, which is good because you need to tuck the nose and the beard/mustache/hair up under the hat.

There are two ways to complete this next step. You can go ahead and tack the hat with a stitch or two on each side (don't glue because the glue takes up too much room) and tuck the hair/beard and nose up under one at a time (start with the mustache/beard first), gluing as you go. Or you can measure where the hat will fall, then remove the hat, arrange the nose and hair, and glue them into place when you are satisfied with their positioning. Add and tack the hat last. You will understand the benefits of each method if you try both ways. If you will be making many gnomes, figuring out which assembly steps are easiest for you will make the process of putting many little people together easier.

I finished my gnome by stuffing more fiber into the hat and allowing some of the polyester or cotton stuffing to stick out for a frizzy hair look. You can glue this hair into place for a firmer hold. Trim beard and hair for the finishing touch with sharp scissors.

Remember, if you make a mess with the glue gun, don't scrap the project out of frustration. With a pair of sharp scissors, you can easily remove unsightly blobs or even carefully shave the glue off the surface of the felt. Just take a deep breath, focus, and concentrate on your gnome glue-grooming. He will look magnificent!

A MAGNIFICENT GNOME AT YOUR SERVICE

Spirit Fairy
pattern on page 228

The spirit fairy is one of my favorite enchanted dolls because the premise is a connection to the divinity in nature. You can make a spirit fairy for every plant, every tree, every weed, every stone—the choices are more than any of us could create in a lifetime. You can also make fairies for emotions: the love fairy, the healing fairy, the confidence fairy, the change fairy—again, there is no end to your creativity! You can fashion the fairy out of one fabric print, sew several prints together and then cut out the doll, or you can simply use muslin or a plain fabric, stuff the doll, and then glue printed fabric swatches on the body.

For adults who will receive the doll, I often use straight pins as part of the embellishment process as they function to hold something on (such as the hair or earrings) and look decorative as well. I take care in their placement as you don't want them to jag the recipient of the doll; I always glue them in place, and sometimes I cut the pins down to ensure they won't come out of the other side of the doll. I don't use pin embellishments for dolls that go to children.

MANY OF MY DOLLS ALSO COME WITH LONG HAT PINS,
DECORATED SAFETY PINS, OR NEEDLES DECORATED WITH BEADS
SO THAT THE OWNER CAN PIN A PAPER PETITION TO THE DOLL

Recovery Dolly

patterns on pages 237–239

I created the recovery dolly (or spirit dolly) as an aid in the advancement of healing for someone recovering from illness, whether that be illness or disruption of body, mind, or spirit. I often choose the individual's favorite colors and make sure that the heart packet contains healing herbs and gems specifically for the type of healing necessary.

Charms chosen for the outside of the doll usually correspond to items or activities that the individual loves or that carry the symbolism of a particular type of healing.

THERE IS NO END TO THE SELECTION OF EMBELLISHMENTS
FOR ANY OF YOUR CREATIONS; THIS ONE INCLUDES METAL
CHARMS (ANKH AND A HEART WITH WINGS), BEADWORK, A
CHAIN BELT, A KEY TO OPEN THE WAY, A STAR FOR SUCCESS,
AND A PEACOCK IRON-ON PATCH FOR PROTECTION

Painted Fabric Poppets and Magickal Animals

I have designed a number of unique painted and grunged dolls and spirit animals over the years. (A grunged poppet is painted with tea or coffee, rubbed with spices, and baked—I go into the grunging process in chapter 2.) I have found great pleasure in creating these images and sharing them with friends, family, and customers on my website and in my Etsy store. Bats, cats, cows, ravens…I've sewn, painted, and decorated a number of one-of-a-kind spirit dolls.

When I create a doll or animal, I first design it on graph paper. The next step is to make a prototype out of muslin fabric. I often draw right on the muslin with a pen or pencil and just sew on the lines I have drawn, rather than cutting out pattern pieces, which is time-consuming and tedious. Once the doll is sewn, I turn it right-side out and hard-stuff it with polystuffing. In hard stuffing, you pack the doll tight with small amounts of stuffing. This takes longer but gives you a firmer, more stable product in the end. It is during this stage where I learn whether or not the doll design is a viable one, and it's where I make changes to the pattern. What a doll looks like flat is not necessarily how the doll will appear when it becomes three dimensional. Many times I find that I have to adjust seam lines to make the poppet more pleasing to the eye. Each doll has usually gone through at least three prototypes before I settle on a design I like.

When I make and design spirit animal dolls, I spend several days or weeks on researching the animal—what it eats, where it normally lives, its general "spirit" personality, legends associated with the animal, its socialization process, etc. I have found that the animal often appears in my life in some way. I will hear about the species in the news or I might see the animal in the wild or I may be gifted with a replica of that animal. When these signs appear, I know I am on the right track and that I should continue with my creation. When I finish a spirit animal doll, I either give a food offering to nature or I contribute in some way to the welfare of that type of animal through a monetary donation.

When I finally have a design I like for any of my creations, I machine stitch most of my designs with a smaller than normal stitch length. This way, the seams don't break loose when I'm stuffing the doll. When I first began creating my dolls, I used the normal stitch length and double-stitched all the seams, but this took way too much time. I decided to employ the smaller stitch length, which works very well. Before I sew the spirit doll shut, I always include some sort of "come alive" packet to breathe life into the doll (see chapter 3). This packet might be a small bag of a different color filled with particular herbs or things I have gathered from nature for a specific intent, a material envelope I have sewed, or merely wrapping the sigil and a gemstone blessed with magickal oil and fluid condenser tightly in a strip of cloth. As I mentioned earlier, I always light a match and drop the lit match into the doll. This is to put the breath of life and the fire of love into the doll. Every packet is different because every doll is unique.

In this book I have provided you with some of my special animal designs. All of my designs were initially made out of muslin, stuffed, and painted with acrylic paints. For a softer effect on the painted muslin animals, I lightly sand the bodies with light grit sandpaper. For Painted Pony, I needle-felted merino wool onto the pony for the mane and tail. His eyes are metal brads affixed with fabric glue. To make the wool easier to handle, I twisted it tightly first and then needle-felted it in place. Painted Pony was designed for motivation, moving forward, and removing blocks in your life. I made two versions—one painted red (which I still have; see the photo on the very first page of this book) and another painted a rich, buttery golden yellow for success.

The animal designs can be as complicated or as simple as you desire. They work well with several mediums, including paper, wax, felt, and muslin. I have constructed all the animals out of muslin and grunged and painted the designs. For a faster process without the grunging, use felt. Many times I use brads or buttons for the eyes, although on occasion I paint the eyes freehand.

Painted Pony
pattern on page 255

This design is for movement in your life, speed, messages, transportation, and tribal matters. Painted Pony, depending upon the intent you have set for him, traverses the heavens in a sha-monic state, bringing you the information and power needed to accomplish a set task or work through a problem. In lore, he/she can bring you wisdom, the power to lead, and the ability to heal.

I use a hard stuffing technique on most of my animals and grunged dolls, including Painted Pony. The method requires packing the stuffing in the image very tightly. It takes much longer to fill your creature (for example it can take an hour to stuff two doll legs); but, the result is well worth it. Your creation is firm, making a pleasing appearance, and is also easier to paint. For the pony, leave the hooves open and insert sticks gathered from the woods after the animal is stuffed. Many times I carve runes on the twigs, slather the top third with glue, and then slide the sticks into the body. Once I'm satisfied with the placement, I use pearl embroidery thread, leaving 3 inches free at the beginning, and wrap the thread around the leg opening at least twenty times, or until I feel the stick is stable. Tie the two ends of thread together, knotting securely. Cut remaining thread close to the knot. Add a dab of glue on the knot so it won't unravel. For the mane and tail, I used a needle felting technique, twisting the merino wool fibers to keep them from pulling apart, and then felting the twisted wool with the punch needle to hold mane or tail in place. To complete the magick of this design, I paint a symbol or sigil that matches the intent of the animal on its hip.

To complete the magick of this design, I paint a symbol or sigil that matches the intent of the animal on its hip.

Duck

pattern on page 253

Diaper cakes are very popular these days—the only drawback is the expense of the objects to hang from it! You can make both the bunnies on page 182 and the ducks (without the eyes) out of colorful fabric for mom to share with baby, or you can make your ducks and bunnies out of felt to place on baby shower gifts as part of the décor. If the animals go to baby, bless a heart-shaped piece of fabric and stuff in the body of the animal to ensure your creation is safe. This type of creation is considered an ornie (ornament) in the doll-making world.

The ducks in the picture are painted and grunged. Their heart packets are filled with bringing good fortune to the owner. This type of creation is often displayed in a basket or used as a decorative shelf-sitter. Ducks and swans often symbolize a happy marriage.

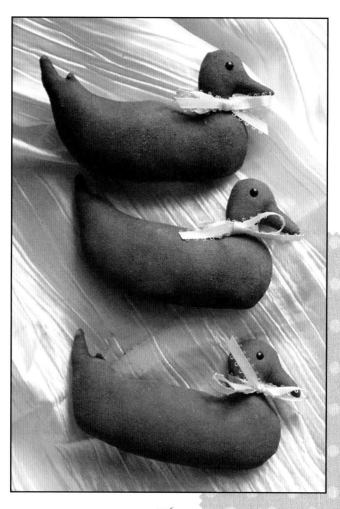

Kitten Prim

pattern on page 260

These kitties are part of my lucky black cat ornie design collection. Each kitty's heart packet can contain good fortune herbs, a petition of luck, and a jade gemstone. Every time the bell rings, good fortune is on its way!

Good Fortune Magick Cat

pattern on page 249

The idea of creating good fortune magick cats (of which I have designed several different patterns) came from the lucky black cat formulas of the Hoodoo world, where the focus is drawing money through risk, gambling, and good luck. There are quite a few traditional blends, depending on the practitioner. To me, moving forward in life is always a risk (a delightful one, but a chance taken nonetheless). Cat's energy is associated with agility and independence—two highly prized gifts in the spirit world. I use various good fortune blends and sigils in my cats, letting intuition guide the way as I construct the individual animal.

Many prosperity gemstones and crystals will fit very well in your good fortune cat. Choose those that you feel belong in the body of your creature (or in the heart packet). I personally like bloodstone, jade, and citrine. Many of my cats have a carved or paper fish, catnip, and feathers added to their heart packets, along with an herbal good fortune mixture. These are general favorites of cats, added to bring them joy. One lucky black cat herbal formula I use in my creatures, mainly if they are to bring good fortune through my own creativity, contains cinnamon, bay, allspice, nutmeg, sassafras, Jezebel root, and patchouli.

Medicine Bear
pattern on page 248

Bear energy travels through the heart and soul of healing, herbal medicine, and protection, often through travel. In January 1978 a massive blizzard hit from Philly to Boston, and I was driving in it with my yellow Camero. I was petrified. I drove from south-central Pennsylvania to Massachusets. (Did I say I was stupid? Yeah, that too.) As I drove (with a cat in the car, mind you), I passed stuck tractor trailers, wrecked and stalled cars, and pickup trucks facing the wrong way—and I motored forward, ever onward. Not only was that trip a physical nightmare, it was a massive mental terror as well. It was the first time I employed the help of spirit animals, and that is why the experience will be locked in my mind forever. I visualized six larger-than-life polar bears chuffing along on either side of my vehicle, getting me through that mess where the snow was so high that it covered the roadside signs. Years later I found myself lost and alone on a highway during another horrendous snowstorm. Once again I called upon my polar bears. They didn't let me down. I made it home safe, albeit fingers stiff from gripping the steering wheel and my legs wobbly from hours of tense sitting while circling in the dark.

I regularly use amethyst, aquamarine, and moonstone for travel protection sachets and animals. My healing bears always have a quartz crystal either attached to the outside of the animal or in the heart packet inside the body, as quartz crystal is called the Master Healer. I also

use osha root in the creature (although it smells awful), depending upon the sickness. Bears battle the pattern of illness. My herbal mix for most of my bears includes borage, white sage, peppermint, eucalyptus, cedar, and beeswax.

Bird Prim
pattern on page 252

The best way to work with the energy of spirit animals is to experience their behavior through personal observation on a repetitive basis. Those creatures that are an integral part of your habitat will share the most information if you only allow them to do so, and what you receive may not be what you've read in books. For example, the owl is often associated with death; however, I have not found this message in my experience. I live in the woods. There are owls. Every time an owl hoots at night or wings through the air across from my porch, someone is not going to drop dead. For me, I have found the owl to mean "the mysteries"—learning, opportunity in knowledge and wisdom, and whether or not there is magick afoot that somehow might involve myself or my loved ones. Likewise, in my world, the crow lets me know if someone is stirring up trouble. Crows are frequent visitors to my backyard and often do so quietly. They strut around in my magick circle. Sometimes they eat the peanuts I leave for them and other times they don't. If their visit is noisy, I know that someone is plotting or attempting to bring negativity into my family unit. They are the ultimate messenger of balance—the crow/raven walks between the worlds. When the crow delivers the message, which you acknowledge, you then give them a missive in return, telling the crow/raven to carry the power to disrupt the negativity. Address the bird with honor, and you will be granted the same.

A nice mixture for inclusion with crows/ravens includes crushed peanut shells, eyebright, spearmint, dill, and vervain. If you wish information from the human spirit world, add grave dirt gathered from a favored ancestor's resting place. Lapis lazuli, turquoise, amethyst, crystal, and moonstone are all excellent choices to adorn these powerful spirit birds.

Brigid's Bunny
pattern on page 250

Brigid's Bunny is dedicated to the goddess Brigid and her creative and healing gifts. Brigid is also the goddess of herbal power and midwifery. A perfect gift for an expectant mother or as a protector in the room of a new baby, this rabbit is machine stitched using cotton muslin, then painted when completed.

After stitching, turn rabbit inside-out and stuff with organic cotton and offerings sacred to the goddess Brigid, such as: dried grains, 8 pennies, 9 white pebbles, oak leaves, willow bark, lambs wool, hazel nuts, hops, rosemary, dill, chamomile, and clover. Stitch closed. Paint body white. Paint the eyes. Grunge with coffee, cinnamon, and allspice. Add a fluffy white pom-pom for the tail and organza ribbon. Empower in a ceremony using red and white candles on a new moon; best on Imbolc.

Bunnie Ornie
pattern on page 251

Although bunnies and rabbits are associated with the spring season, birth, procreation, and just downright being adorable, their medicine for survival is the most powerful of all. There is nothing that will fight harder for life (or be more creative in that instinct) than the rabbit. When stuffing your creature, don't be deceived by the idea that something so cute and cuddly is inherently weak or consistently fearful—quite the opposite. A healer's gift of a rabbit spirit animal to someone who is ill is an offering of strength, endurance, and creativity in survival.

Herbs for your heart packet for an adult healing might include damiana, mistletoe, bay, olive leaf, black tea, and woodruff. For a child, remove the damiana, mistletoe, and woodruff, as those should not be ingested. Turritella agate, with its pattern of fossilized shell in the stone, can be included for survival, wisdom, and overall healing.

Stuff these cute little creatures with natural cotton and wishing herbs. Add a large amount of dried chocolate mint to the stuffing and paint them brown to make the chocolate bunnies you see here. Use metal brads with a bit of glue for the eyes. Finish with a bit of organza ribbon for a lovely spring gift. For an expectant mother, you could paint them blue or white, then stuff them with chamomile, cotton, and a petition for safe delivery.

Taco Cat

patterns on pages 258 & 259

My Taco Cat and his lady friend, Sriracha Cat (same pattern—you just make her a skirt; see her on the very first page of this book), have become leading figures in my poppet construction. Fun and loveable, Taco Cat took on a personality totally his own.

His name is derived from the spices I used to grunge him—taco spices! Little did I realize when I designed him just what an amazing energy he would add to my life. Larger than many of my other projects, Taco Cat has made regular appearances on my Instagram, Facebook, and Twitter feeds. Taco Cat absolutely represents the spice of life: loving adventure, having a sense of humor, being courageous. His geist bag holds toys, rose quartz, a crystal, taco spices, hot

peppers from my garden, a ghost pepper that I was told was so hot it would kill a person (no kidding), coffee beans, tonka beans, 3 pennies, a match, and a "come alive" paper charm.

For quite a while I posted interesting pics of Taco Cat frequently, but then doubt set in and I thought, "Maybe I should stop making such a fuss over this stuffed cat." So I did. What I didn't expect were all the posts and emails asking me what the heck happened to Taco Cat! One email I received made up my mind about Taco Cat and sharing his pattern here. I'll paraphrase:

"Dear Silver, I just wanted you to know how much my mother and I love seeing the pictures of Taco Cat that you post. My mother is dying of cancer, and every day she asks about Taco Cat so she can see a funny picture and laugh."

After I got done bawling my eyes out, I posted another pic of Taco Cat having a good time. Taco Cat stands for never giving up and never giving in to stupid stuff. Eventually I posted story pics of Taco Cat looking for and meeting Sriracha Cat (his lady friend). I had so much fun thinking up ideas for their big meeting. I even had Sriracha Cat cast a spell to "catch her cat" (so to speak). Sriracha Cat is all about independence and personal empowerment. Her geist bag contains a teeny-weeny statue of Sekhmet, dragon's blood resin, hot peppers, coffee, a tiny bottle of perfume, and a "come alive" paper charm.

Taco Cat represented a learning experience on many levels. I learned that once muslin material is painted and grunged, it is very difficult to add eyes, mouth, etc., by stitching. You'll dance with sore fingers and several broken needles—and, if you are like me, a pointed explicative or two (or a hundred). To avoid this heightened irritation, I stitched the mouth onto the cat before I painted it and glued on the eyes and the eyelids after the cat was painted and grunged. To secure the nose and eyelids, I pinned them on with straight pins dipped in E6000 glue. I rarely use glue on my dolls (because glue is untrustworthy for a long-lasting product), but with Taco Cat using glue became part of the design structure to keep the eyes, eyelids, and nose in place. I wanted the eyes to be unusual and whimsical, so I stacked and glued together colored buttons. For both cats I used merino wool, twisting strands together and needle felting the twists to the heads with a sharp serrated needle made for this purpose.

If you make one of these cats, prepare for your life to change!

Swan Ornie

pattern on page 256

Swan's power lies in transformation, rising above the sticky net of our own negative thoughts and swimming freely in the sea of potential. Swan reminds us that we have the inherent ability to change in a way that brings us joy and provides happiness for others. Many believe that the swan energy enhances psychic abilities and heightened perception. The swan's association to love and partnership traces from Greek (Aphrodite) and Roman (Venus) mythology and alludes to love; however, swan's greatest gift is the ferocity in which she protects her young, and consequently the association with protection of the general family. Double swans signify the unity of family—the power and protection of the clan.

Protective herbs for the heart packet can include juniper berries, cedar, rosemary, yarrow flowers, cinquefoil, and basil. Include labradorite if you think someone sends evil intentions, blue kyanite to stop bullies and manipulation, or black obsidian to break curses.

Sweet Sleep Sheep

patterns on pages 246 & 247

There are just some animals you adore because of their cultural or daily life associations. The sheep is one of those creatures, associated with sweet sleep, rest, peaceful surroundings, warmth, and environmental security. In the real world, if sheep are happily grazing, the dog has kept the evil away. I designed my sheep spirit animals as vehicles for restful sleep and dream solutions, experimenting with different formulas until I found the ones that were most useful to my energy vibration. Over the years I've learned that one herbal blend doesn't fit the energy patterns of all people. The best way to work with the herbs is to start with the base recipe and then study the results as you add or remove different ingredients until you have something that works well for you.

This sheep pattern is easy to construct and works well with different material choices. Over the years I've used muslin, pieced cotton, felt, foam, and paper. My choice of supplies often rests on the amount of time available to make the project and how long I want the project to last. The sheep in the photographs were sewn out of unbleached cotton and then painted with acrylics, grunged, and baked in the oven. For years they hung over the headboard of my bed; now they travel with me to my poppet seminars. The painting and grunging process takes the most time; however, these sheep have weathered the years well! If you are using felt, foam, or paper, the sheep goes together very quickly, but it probably won't last very long.

THESE SHEEP WERE CONSTRUCTED WITH MACHINE-STITCHED
MUSLIN, ACRYLIC PAINT, AND A GRUNGING FORMULA;
THEIR EYES ARE METAL BRADS INSERTED WITH A BIT OF
GLUE ON THE ENDS, AND THE EARS ARE BLACK FELT

If someone is having difficulty sleeping, add a protective sigil or angel association inside the sheep. A bell can be inserted inside or stitched outside as a symbol of warning and energy clearing to keep the sleeping individual safe. One of the things I like best about this pattern is that you can make lots of little sheep or go for the gusto and make a big sheep! The design lends itself well to resizing. Another option is to add a piece of decorative cloth as a blanket for your sheep. You can slip a special petition under the blanket before you sew or glue the blanket into place.

Gemstones associated with sweet sleep include selenite, quartz crystal, rose quartz, moonstone, jade, dalmatian jasper, and celestite. Stick to tumbled stones for sleep magick rather than points. For restful sleep, try a combination of amethyst, rose quartz, selenite, and celestite. For dream solutions, combine jade, quartz crystal, danburite, and moonstone. Lepidolite, dalmatian jasper, chrysoprase, red jasper, turquoise, and black tourmaline are thought to assist in dispelling nightmares. Add these stones in any combination (or alone) to your sheep.

Enhance the power of the sheep by blending your gemstone choices with a dried herbal mix. For example, eyebright and lavender herbs combined with ametrine, strawberry quartz, and red jasper are used in dream recall.

Herbals associated with sweet sleep include aniseed, balsam fir, calendula, chamomile, cloves, hops, lavender, lemon balm, lemongrass, lemon verbena, lilac, marjoram, mimosa, mint, mugwort, passionflower, rose, rosemary, and thyme.

I have several sleep sheep herbal and gemstone combinations that you may find useful:

Sheep in the Meadow (for General Dreams of Well-Being and Restful Sleep): Lavender, kava-kava, rosemary, and vetiver with turquoise gemstone (for eliminating stress).

Sweet Sleep Sheep (for Dreams of Magick and Happiness): Mugwort, lavender, and hops combined with hematite gemstone.

Baa-Baa Bliss (for Dreams of Peace): Rose, rosemary, lavender, hops, and balsam coupled with black tourmaline and red jasper.

Healing Flock (for Recuperating Sleep During or After Illness): Lavender, mugwort, marjoram, mint, catnip, rose, hibiscus herbs, with rose quartz and howlite gemstones. I chose this gemstone combination because when you are recovering from sickness, there is wisdom gained from your illness. In my opinion, howlite will help you capture this information so you don't have to go through it again!

Dog in Sheep's Clothing (to Protect You During the Sleep Cycle): Lepidolite, dalmatian jasper, chrysoprase, and black tourmaline combined with juniper berries, frankincense, hops, passion flower, valerian, ginseng, skullcap, cayenne, chamomile, and lemon balm. Please remember that nightmares are signals that you have issues you need to address. Seek qualified assistance if your bad dreams are persistent or if you are feeling overwhelmed.

Loving Lamb (for Dreams of Love): Rose, rosemary, lemon verbena, mint, cloves, calendula petals, and catnip. Add cayenne peppers for thoughts of passion. Gemstone choices can include rose quartz, moonstone, and lapis lazuli.

Prosperity Pig

pattern on page 254

Often connected to women's mysteries, the pig (swine, sow, boar) weaves its magick throughout the myths of humankind. Symbolizing abundance, fertility, and good fortune, the pig's energy links to intelligence, endurance, wealth through agriculture, unleashing one's inspiration, and feeding artistic ability. Piggy's geist bag contains sunflower seeds; gold or silver coins; moonstone, carnelian, bloodstone, and chrysoprase gemstones; sassafras, chamomile, and allspice herbs; and dirt from three prosperous businesses (check out those places before you use the dirt).

Cute rounded ears for animals are easy to make if you remember to fold the bottom seam under (after you turn the ear right-side out) and then pinch the bottom closed. Secure with a stitch or two and you have a cloth piece that actually looks like an ear. I also insert a small section of pipe cleaner into the tail, then place the open end of the tail (free of pipe cleaner so you don't break your needle) along the edge of the right side of the fabric before sewing the front and back of the pig together. Baste to hold. Put the second side of the pig on top of the first (right sides together). Stitch around the the pig. (The tail is nestled inside the body of the pig between the two pieces of fabric.) When you turn the pig right side out, the tail will be secure in the seam.

I FOUND THESE STAR TAILS AT A CRAFT STORE;

SEE PAGE **173** FOR ANOTHER STYLE OF PROSPERITY PIG

Bat

pattern on page 261

In legend, the bat is about transformation and being able to use the totality of your senses to make your way through transition. Out here in the woods, bats come with messages from the shadow realm at twilight. I was so inspired by watching them dance through the dusk my first summer here that I created this bat pattern. Over the years, the bat has become one of my favorite designs, and if I didn't know what to make but felt crafty, I would stitch up a bat! I guarantee that he will win the hearts of everyone at Halloween!

I've used the bat pattern for muslin, colorful cotton, and felt. Outside stitching (after the bat has been sewn together and turned to the right side) denotes the fingers on the wings. For realistic wings, paint the muslin, allow to dry, and then lightly sand the surface. The wings gain stability and have a fantastic leathery appearance! I've even used this design for bedtime sachets made of quilting cotton, leaving the bottom of the bat open and gluing Velcro to the inside edges so that you can change the herbals every month or so. The bat's geist bag contains dried moonflower leaves, moonflower seeds, dried fruit seeds (like apple, a peach pit, etc.), a wooden carved image of a bug, a match, and a "come alive" sigil. If you have pets that will grab your bat (it happens) or any of your spirit animals, you might want to fill their geist bags with food-safe ingredients rather than what I have listed here.

The bat pattern lends itself well to cotton and machine stitching or felt and a glue gun. For machine stitching, lay the pattern directly on the cloth, secure with a few pins, and stitch around the pattern using the edges of paper as your guide. Remember to leave an opening at the bottom for turning and stuffing. Wing stitching for segments is done after the bat has been turned inside right.

PRIMITIVE BAT (TOP) AND DREAMBAT (BOTTOM)

Gargoyle

patterns on pages 262 & 263

In magick and enchantments I use the gargoyle for its protective energies. The geist bag for my gargoyles often contains juniper berries, a silver pentacle, a bullet casing packed with black salt, cloves, black onyx, smoky quartz, and amethyst gemstones, and seven-cemetery dirt (dirt gathered from the graves of seven ancestors in seven different cemeteries) or the dirt from the grave of a bravely famous soldier, along with the "come alive" paper charm.

To keep the gargoyle wings stable, I insert double pipe cleaners in the wings after I have turned the animal right-side out. I then tack-stitch on the outside close to the pipe cleaner edges so they won't slip. Once the gargoyle is painted, grunged, and sanded, you don't notice the stitching. Like the bat, I don't stuff the wings, preferring the leathery appearance of the painted, sanded surface. Adjust the length of the tail to your liking by extending the straight portion of the pattern.

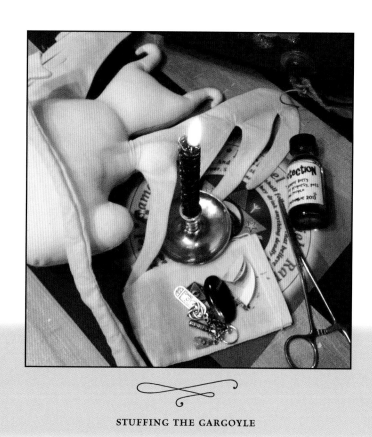

STUFFING THE GARGOYLE

Basket of Bones Ornies
pattern on page 242

I designed the basket of bones pattern to fulfill two functions: to bring positive energies into the home during the fall season and as a divination tool for our Samhain celebrations. The skull and bones fit well into a decorative basket and can also be a centerpiece for your Halloween party and other late autumn social functions. I used the primitive grunging technique in their creation because I wanted the energies of the coffee/cinnamon solution to be part of my overall working. The result of the white paint smudged with the herbal formula makes the skull and bones look graveyard worthy.

I began by sewing the pieces out of muslin, stuffing each one with a specialized herb sachet dipped in universal fluid condenser, then painting the bones white, adding the wording and facial design in black, and finally rubbing the skull and bones with a coffee/cinnamon solution. You can make as many bones as you desire. I made five bones and a head for the original pattern. Each bone is a magical sachet dedicated to an energy type, complete with herbal formula and specialized sigil for the energy that the bone represents.

EACH BONE HAS ITS OWN PROPERTIES AND ENERGY TYPE

The following ingredients are what I used in several of my projects of this type. Feel free to change the formulas to what will suit you best.

Wealth: Sunflower seeds, bay leaves with dollar signs drawn on them, chamomile, peppermint, sassafras, lavender, patchouli, and one bloodstone.

Protection: Eggshell, rosemary, lemon verbena, larkspur, white sage, and one onyx.

Love: Rose petals, African basil, ginger root, cinnamon, licorice root, orange peel, hot peppers, and one rose quartz tumbled stone.

Mysteries (Messages from the Dead): Mint, marjoram, wormwood, eyebright, grave dirt, patchouli, and one quartz crystal.

Healing: Dandelion root, rosemary, acorn, dogwood, lemon verbena, eucalyptus, kava-kava, osha root, and one amethyst stone.

The Head: Dirt of your ancestors' graves or seven-cemetery dirt, rose petals, white sage, eyebright, sandalwood, lavender, rosemary, frankincense, and myrrh. For stones, celestite, charoite, phenacite, angelite, blue lace agate, and selenite all have spiritual associations for speaking to the beloved dead, angels, and higher energy forms.

The biggest challenge was painting the right wording on its corresponding bone, as once they were stuffed, I had no idea what herbal formula was in which bone! To keep from making a mistake, I pinned the name on the bone until I was ready to paint it. I also made a page in my magickal journal about how I created the project so I could remember what ingredients I used.

For divination purposes, the participant is asked to close their eyes and choose a bone from the basket. The bone they choose represents the energy they need most in their lives right now. You can have the same labeled herbal ingredients you used to create the project on a tray so that the person can make a conjure bag/sachet to take with them. For example, if they chose the healing bone, you would hand them the healing herbs mix you have previously prepared and a conjure bag. Instruct them to add a lock of their hair to the bag and carry it with them for healing until Yule. On Yule (Winter Solstice) they should burn the bag outdoors in a ceremony of release and healing.

THIS SET CAN BE USED IN ANCESTRAL CELEBRATIONS
FOR MANY YEARS, IF YOU SO CHOOSE—THE MORE
RITUALS, THE GREATER THE POWER!

Chakra Fish
pattern on page 257

A chakra is a point of energy or energy center within the auric and physical body that is thought to spin. Each center is like a portal that can be used to heal the body and enhance our daily lives. Although popular material focuses on only seven centers (those that operate within the trunk of the body), there are many more. Even animals have a chakra system that is much like ours but carries an additional point at the shoulders. I developed chakra fish spirit animals as an aid in meditation and hands-on healing. I chose the fish vehicle because I see them as energy that flows into and through the sea of potential all around us. In my private yoga practice, I sometimes pin a fish to my clothing or line them up at the front or side of my mat. If I am ill, I hold the fish that corresponds to the blocked chakra on my body. I have also formed a ring of the spirit fish around an individual's picture or lock of hair. These spirit dolls can be laid on the body at the matching energy point or lined up on a petition. Their uses are endless in the realm of healing and energy work. I have even used them as divination tools when I am uncertain what energy center(s) are blocked. I put all the fish in a paper bag and then concentrate on the question "Which chakra point needs to be attended to today?"—then pull out a fish. I can then tailor my work not only to the associations of that energy center, but I also use that color correspondence in candle magick.

As a note, there is also a twelve-chakra system, with four above the seven indicated here and one below—a root that communicates like the roots of a tree. Those above the crown deal with transcending time, the soul, using your mind over matter, and uniting with the All (universal spirit). For more information on using your spirit dolls as chakra healers, you may be interested in Cyndi Dale's book *The Complete Book of Chakra Healing: Activate the Transformative Power of Your Energy Centers.*

In the list below, you will find suggested colors, gemstones, and herb formulas for the basic seven chakra fish and one very special fish, the ghost fish, who is the protector of all the other fish. His function is to dispel evil and negativity and to banish nasty spirits while the healer is working. Keep in mind that the formulas you use are subject to your intuition. There are many practitioners who match herbs by color rather than aroma, medicinal use, or taste—for example, the sacral chakra, which is orange, would relate to orange flowers, fruits, or spices (tiger lily, orange, etc.). Gemstones are often chosen the same way. You can select one gemstone to put in the doll or chips of several different stones. Adding an empowered "come alive" slip of paper in the doll also aids in its overall energy form. As I constructed my fish, I chanted the sound associated with that chakra point. Feel free to experiment! These little dollies/fishes are your "A" healing team!

For this project, felt, embroidery thread, glass beads, and my glue gun functioned as my go-to tools for construction. I embellished both sides of the fish separately, then loaded the herbs and gemstones in the center of one half, using the glue gun to hold the items in place. Finally, gluing a bit at a time, I placed one half of the fish over the other and slowly closed the body. The nice thing about a hot glue gun and felt is that if you have very sharp scissors, you can trim away any mess you have made during the construction.

My chakra fish collection took me seven days to complete and was begun over a new moon cycle. I didn't plan it that way—sometimes the creative process, particularly if it is mixed with magick, moves forward at its own pace.

Ghost Fish: White. Protection, banish evil spirits, dissolve negativity. Tridarna gemstone and frankincense resin.

Crown Chakra: "I Am." Purple. Wisdom, spirit, enlightenment and transcendence, source energy. *Herbal Formula:* lavender (this herb is thought to work well for all energy points of the body), dried lotus flowers, gotu kola. *Gemstones:* amethyst, diamond, clear quartz, selenite. *Sound:* Om.

Third Eye Chakra: "I Know." Indigo. Perception, intuition, inspiration. *Herbal Formula*: eyebright, spearmint, juniper, mugwort, rosemary, poppy, lemon, lavender. *Gemstones*: amethyst, purple flourite, labradorite, black obsidian. *Sound*: Sham.

Throat Chakra: "I Speak." Blue. Truth, expression, communication. *Herbal Formula*: clover, lemon balm, eucalyptus, salt, lemongrass, peppermint, coltsfoot, white sage. *Gemstones*: aquamarine, lapis lazuli, sodalite, turquoise, aventurine, amazonite, blue chalcedony. *Sound*: Ham.

Heart Chakra: "I Love." Green. Heart, compassion, love. *Herbal Formula*: hawthorne, marjoram, rose, basil, thyme, sage, cilantro, jasmine, parsley, cayenne. *Gemstones*: green tourmaline, jade, rose quartz, adventurine, strawberry quartz, green calcite. *Sound*: Yam.

Solar Plexus Chakra: "I Do." Yellow. Power, will, socialization, ego, impulse. *Herbal Formula*: lavender, bergamot, rosemary, mint, ginger, fennel, marshmallow, celery, lily, lemon balm, anise. *Gemstones*: orange calcite, citrine, sunstone, red agate, topaz. *Sound*: Ram.

Sacral Chakra: "I Feel." Orange. Emotions, creativity, sexuality, self-worth. *Herbal Formula*: sandalwood, calendula, licorice, cinnamon, paprika, gardenia, sesame, coriander, hibiscus, vanilla. *Gemstones*: carnelian, sunstone, snowflake obsidian, citrine, coral, moonstone. *Sound*: Vam.

Root Chakra: "I Am." Red. Earth connection, survival instinct, grounding. *Herbal Formula*: dandelion, kava kava, cloves, burdock, valerian root, elderflowers. *Gemstones*: red agate, bloodstone, black tourmaline, hematite, garnet, red aventurine, onyx, smokey quartz, tiger's eye. *Sound*: Lam.

Chakra fish will take on their own personalities the more you use them. They like to be kept together, even if you are only using one of them. You can make individual chakra poppets to heal friends and family and give them as gifts. If, however, you make a set for a specific intention (such as healing or transformation), I've found that breaking them up diminishes their power. Now and then one of them may wander off—that happens. Call it back while playing "seek-and-go-find" and you should find it quickly. A missing fish means that you need to pay attention to that energy center in your own body. Once you acknowledge this, it is easier to find the fish!

Cleanse your chakra poppets after every use by sprinkling them with salt or an herbal mixture of your choice (lavender, rosemary, sage, and basil are good choices). I sage my fish on the dark of the moon and re-energize them on the new moon. Sometimes I also use a strong astrological event for a special ritual with them. I recommend that you keep your chakra poppets in a special bag or box laced with a protective herb sachet or wooden rune pieces.

Note: There are several healing charts for dogs, cats, and horses on the internet, should you be interested in that subject. Animals have eight major chakras, twenty-one minor, and six "bud" energy points. It is thought that animal chakras are far brighter than human chakras. The eighth chakra mentioned earlier is called the brachial chakra and is located around the shoulder blades. Its associated color is black. This chakra is considered the primary energy point for animals and stands for the relationship between the animal and humans. Gemstones for this point include tiger's-eye, snowflake obsidian, carnelian, and black gemstones in general.

STUFFING FOR CHAKRA FISH

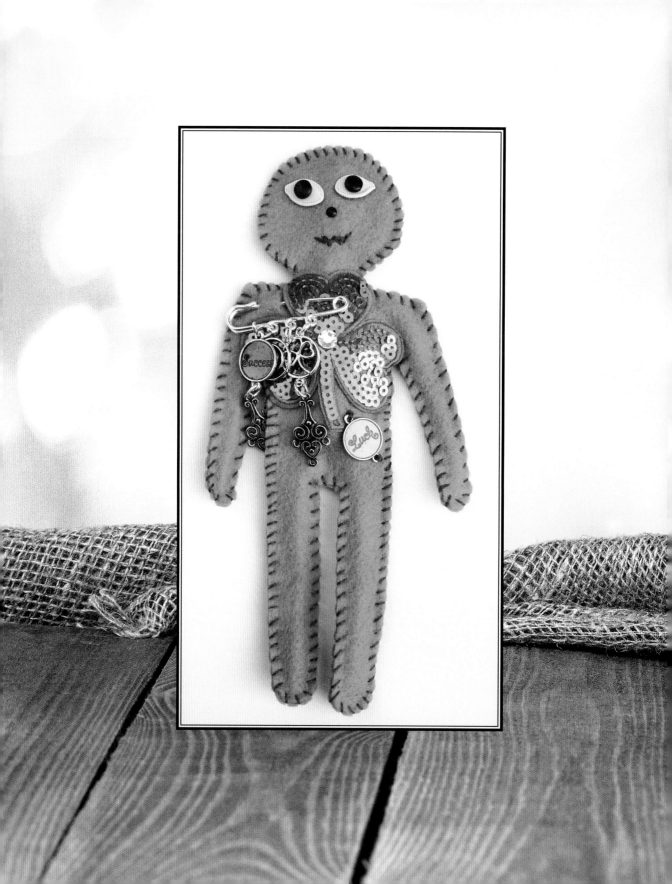

six

Handling Your Spirit Dolls

Taking Care of Your Permanent Poppets

Permanent poppets, such as those for family members, deity representations, or house spirits, may be used many times in magick. To keep the energy focused, process only one petition (or command) at a time with the doll. I realize that you may have many, many requests, but the more conduits you have open, the more chance of the energy becoming weakened. If there are so many problems you simply don't know where to start, work for joy or clarity of mind (whichever you feel is more appropriate). You can also use a family member doll as a central focus, and place your petitions or requests in a conjuring bag, envelope, or cloth packet that is not physically attached to the doll. In this scenario, the doll would not be activated to "do" something; it is merely a representation of the recipient, giving a conduit for your work to travel easily to that person.

In rural Pennsylvania around the 1850s, women made colorful pockets out of quilted material to wear around their waist. These pockets carried any number of items and were held together around the body with a cord. You can use this concept by stitching a small apron with pockets for your doll or simply making a unique pocket to tie around the doll with string.

Just as with other magickal tools, the permanent doll should be kept in a sacred place and cleansed after the desire has been met. Cleansing can include clearing with sage or incense, holy water, chants and charms for cleansing, placing the doll in a bowl of salt overnight, or putting it in the direct rays of the sun or moon for several hours. Dolls or poppets that have a single mission, such as a doll for protection, should be cleansed and re-activated once a month, preferably at the same time—meaning if you originally empowered the doll on the full moon, then the next empowerment should be as close to a full moon as possible.

BEER AND CAKES OFFERED TO THE HOUSE SPIRITS ON FASCHNAUT
DAY, THE PENNSYLVANIA DUTCH TRADITION OF MAKING
POTATO-BASED DONUTS FRIED IN LARD ON SHROVE TUESDAY

If you set your poppets out all the time, they will gather negativity and dirt. Unless the doll is on display for a magickal reason, keep your poppet in a sacred place, away from prying eyes and sticky fingers. Wrapping your poppet in white or black cloth adds a level of protection—putting it in a safe magickal box is also an excellent idea. If poppets that have been used in magick are left lying around unattended, they will get into trouble, and on occasion this energy inverts the power of the poppet, causing disruptions in the home. If this occurs, cleanse and bless the poppet, then cover it in black or white cloth for at least seven days. If crossed conditions continue and you feel the doll is the root of the problem, ritually dispose of the doll, thanking it for its service, and make a new one.

Making Poppets for Others

You may wish to make a poppet for a close friend or perhaps you like constructing poppets so much that you want to sell them. In my experience, never make a poppet when you are sick, angry, or depressed, as this energy will be infused in the doll. As its creator, you have ultimate power over what goes into the poppet. It doesn't matter that the doll has left your hands. Your birth energy is still there, even if you have cleansed the doll appropriately and added the magickal locking mechanism I spoke of earlier (see page 92).

I would like to add here, however, that there are always exceptions to rules. For example, if you have cancer or are plagued with a chronic disease, you can still make very blessed, very good poppets to give to others. When I say "sick," I'm thinking of the flu, a bad cold, the worst hangover ever, or a stomach bug—conditions where your body and your mind are truly scraping rock bottom. Rest is what you need. You can make beautiful poppets later. However, if you are making a poppet while you are ill to destroy the disease (cold, flu, etc.) and plan to dispose of it (preferably by burning it) immediately—it will work just fine. For this emergency-I-am-sick poppet, include a large volume of salt and a little of banishing herbs such as dried olive leaf, rosemary, and white sage as your stuffing. Rub the poppet all over your body. Burn immediately outdoors. If you are too sick to do it yourself, have a trusted family member do it for you.

When giving a poppet to another person, be sure to indicate the initial intent of your work so that the new owner will be in sync with what you have created. Tell them what herbs or charms are in the doll, or better still, write an artful note to go with the doll, listing its purpose and the herbs contained within. Many people don't know what herbs are safe to ingest or handle, nor do they think about the correspondences of those herbs. If the recipient has pets or children and you have included herbs that are considered poisonous, clearly tell the recipient not to allow pets or children near the poppet and why. A puppy using a poppet filled with garden nightshade as a chew toy would be a very, very bad thing indeed! If you are unsure of the safety of an herb, check online. Finally, take into consideration the individual's aromatic likes and dislikes. I know a woman who hates the smell of lavender and won't even buy cleaning products with the scent. Another can't stand patchouli because it reminds her of someone she intensely dislikes, and a man I know is extremely allergic to jasmine. There is nothing worse than giving a poppet that took hours to construct with great care, only to have the new owner wrinkle their nose in distaste at the first sniff or roll on the floor with an acute asthma attack!

Unusual Circumstances

If you fall in love with creating poppets, spirit dolls, and enchanted animals, now and then you are going to experience strange circumstances. For example, I once made a protective doll and "sent" the doll to do its job, which was to turn back the negativity sent to my friend. What I didn't know at the time but learned later is that the individual causing much of the unhappiness had an interesting hobby: that person constructed monster models. My poppet exploded an hour after I "sent" it. (Too bad; it was a neat one.) This is not to say the magick didn't work—it did, and quite well—but know this: any poppet or spirit doll you make has a lifespan, and sometimes it will be over before you expected!

Dollies can also come back to you "wounded." As in the example above, you aren't the only person in the world making dollies, empowering unusual creatures, and employing them in magick. There is an entire fantasy and science fiction community that puts a great deal of power into their creations, yet they know nothing about the real magick like you do. Now and then, one of your permanent dolls may be somehow "off" in energy. It may have been "wounded" after completing its mission and you just didn't notice. Take the time to cleanse, bless, and reconsecrate it. Change its clothing. Give it a new theme. Spruce it up! This is also a signal that you need to do a personal spiritual cleansing—you may be carrying negative energy of which you are unaware.

You may also come to a point where your creations seem to demand something of you—not in a horror story way but in a spiritual light. As they are tied to you because you are their creator, what they need may be something you may also need. For example, maybe you look at your house protection doll one morning and notice that you have a thirsty feeling. What does that mean to you spiritually? Perhaps both you and the doll should do a harmony ritual, a house cleansing, or whatever comes to mind. It is okay and not crazy to communicate and share with your doll in this way. There are days when I cleanse and bless cool water to offer to my dolls. I know that they represent the creative side of myself—and in offering the water, I am paying attention to that part of me that births joy through my art and words. Sometimes I put special foods on the altar and leave for twenty-four hours, or I might add toys, candy, new items of clothing, etc.

Using Storebought Poppets

Many craft stores now offer premade, expressionless muslin/cotton dolls ranging in size from small to large. You can also find kits of wood or foam. Or perhaps you want to do something with a standard doll purchased from a toy store. If you choose to use one of these dolls, I suggest you do a complete cleansing ritual for the doll separately before you perform your normal cleansing with all the supplies (such as additional embellishments, sigils, etc.). Unlike a skein of yarn or a bag of bells, the image form is extremely powerful in itself and has already begun to attract energy simply because of its shape. Manufactured dolls will carry the energy of the place, the workers, the shipping process, the store, and any employees who handled it.

Banishing all negativity is vital before you begin working with a preconstructed doll. Have you ever stood in a checkout line staring at the clerk in horror because they have a horrendous cold and are coughing all over your purchases as they run them through the scanner? You can see that scenario. How about if the clerk just came from a home where there is rampant alcoholism or abuse? They carry that energy with them, too; you just can't see it like the effects of the cold or flu. A magickal cleansing will remove this type of negative energy, ensuring that your doll will perform as you desire. You can also add herbs or a sigil to such a doll by cutting a small slit in the doll's back large enough to handle the insertion of your chosen items. Stitch the doll back up using the whip stitch, then proceed with the birthing ceremony and other magickal rituals you may wish to use.

Molded plastic animals and dolls can also be used in your magickal operations. Cleanse, bless, and consecrate them using the rituals and incantations provided in this book or use your own. I have a complete set of plastic spirit animals on a large shelf in my magickal room. I feed these symbols of the animal kingdom cornmeal and blessed water every day. I ask for their blessings and I use them to communicate with the spirits of these animals and birds. If I need something in particular, like protection for a family member, I will write my request on a piece of paper, draw the sigils I desire on the paper, and anoint with liquid fluid condenser and a magickal oil. Then I set the paper under the animal and ask the animal spirit for assistance. I either leave the paper for twenty-four hours or for seven days, depending on the circumstance, then burn the paper. Normally, the animal stays on the shelf with the others, but now and then I will move it or carry it with me. I also reposition my animals; there are fifty of them at this point. Sometimes the lions like it by the window near the gazelle and other times they would rather be on the sacred rocks.

Once, in desperation, I sent my husband to the store and told him to buy the biggest jug of army men he could find. He thought I was nuts. Maybe I was; however, I used those army men to battle a nasty issue—and I won.

The Mirrored Reversal or Protection Box

The intent of the reversal box is (depending on your wording) to send back or contain negative energy that has been sent to you by a particular individual. A mirrored protection box is to keep a person or animal from harm. The only differences between the two boxes are the ingredients used when making the box, the kind of poppet you choose to put in the box, and the wording when you charm both the box and the poppet. You also need to decide if this box is for a specific poppet and will be destroyed or buried, or if the box will serve for many different reversal or protection spells.

Supplies

- a small box

- black acrylic paint

- sandpaper

- glue

- paintbrush

- mirrors (whole or broken)

- magickal oils and powders to match your intent

- gloss varnish

- acrylic sealer to protect the surface of the paint (optional)

- a prepared poppet

Once you know the intent of your box (reverse or protect), consider magickal timing, just like you would when preparing to make your poppet. Reverse magick does better when the moon is in the third or fourth quarter, when the moon is in Scorpio, or on a Saturday in a Saturn hour. Protection lends itself to the moon in Cancer or on a Monday in the planetary hour of the moon, although you can use the planetary hour of Saturn or the first twelve hours after a new moon—your choice. Gather your supplies, then perform a cleansing and blessing rite.

Once the cleansing and blessing are completed, you are ready to construct the box. With sandpaper, smooth all the edges and surfaces of the box. This is to make the painting job easier and to prevent splinters. As you sand, you may wish to whisper the charm: "Wood and sand I command; as I say, so shall it be," or intone your own chant or charm. Labels from purchased boxes can be pesky. Rather than wetting the label or using a liquid release material, you might try using a very sharp X-Acto knife. Gently insert the blade under one of the edges of the label and work the blade in toward the middle of the label. Turn the box and remove the blade. Insert blade under the opposite corner and work in toward the center. The label should easily pop off. Use the sandpaper to remove any tiny pieces of paper or glue.

The next step is to paint the box inside and out. I always add magickal powders and oils to boost the protective/reversal qualities of the box, and I apply three coats of gloss varnish. After the varnish is dry, empower the mirror pieces. For this box, I said:

> I add these mirrors in the name of Hecate, Queen of Witches, Guardian of the Crossroads, and Commander of the Dead, that their reflection become a cage that will capture all negativity sent to me!

Affix as many mirrors as possible both on the inside and outside of the box with glue. Some practitioners break mirrors and use the shards, fitting them as close together as possible. This is done to help break up negativity.

THIS BOX WAS CONSTRUCTED WITH SEVERAL SIZES OF
MIRRORS; I CHOSE THE PIECES THAT BEST FIT IN THE
BOX. YOU CAN ALWAYS USE TINFOIL INSTEAD.

When the box is completely dry, empower it in a ceremony using black or dark blue candles. For the reversal box, hold the open box in your hands, and say:

> *Hecate, Queen of Witches, Guardian of the Crossroads, and Commander of the*
> *Dead! I call upon thee now to empower this reversal box so that any object placed*
> *within it will be caged in a jungle of reflection, illusion, and confusion so that*
> *whatever lies within may no longer effect any harm!*

You can make your request longer or your intent clearer than what I have written here, or you can leave the specifics for when you lay your chosen poppet in the box, where you will want to call it by name and tell it that it can no longer harm you. The poppet can be bound with wire or twine and sprinkled with magickal herbs to suffocate the harmful individual's power. Likewise, the protection box may hold a poppet of a loved one, the box acting as an enchanted shield of protection. What if you like the idea of this box, but you don't have money for supplies or you need to make something right away and don't have mirrors, etc.? No problem. Using the same idea, cover a small cardboard box or jar inside and out with tinfoil. Just make sure that the container has a lid and that it is also covered with the foil.

Where Do You Go from Here?

Make poppets! Lots of them! Craft them for yourself, your family, and your friends. Send the magick of love, healing, protection, and compassion into the universe! And most importantly, have fun! The next chapter contains twenty-one different poppet formulas. These recipes are just a beginning—a guide to help get you started.

seven

POPPET FORMULAS

As I Craft Thee, So I Wish Thee

The following formulas are those that I have developed over time. Each has its own unique blend focused on a particular life need. Each formula gives recommended herbal or other inclusions, a matching gemstone should you choose to include one, ideas for magickal oils, possible color choices, and recommended timing. All herbs listed are dried. Herbs gathered and dried by yourself, particularly those that are native to your own area, are particularly powerful in poppet magick. The formulas can also be used in conjuring bags, sachets, and enchanted packets.

Love

Herbs: Rose petals, basil, chamomile

Gemstone: Rose quartz

Magickal Oil: Orange blossom, a mixture of jasmine and rose, or an attraction oil of your choice

Color Choices: Red, pink, white

Timing: New moon, first quarter moon, Friday at dawn, in a Venus planetary hour, first or second quarter moon in Scorpio (for sex), on a day when the planet Venus is well aspected

Money

Herbs: Peppermint, lavender, fava beans, sassafras, cinquefoil, dill

Gemstone: Lodestone (dress lodestone with lodestone oil and magnetic sand), bloodstone, moss agate, snowflake obsidian

Other Inclusions: Silver or gold magnetic sand; paper money or three coins in growing denomination

Magickal Oil: Lodestone or money-drawing magickal oil

Color Choices: Green for growth, brown for finding hidden money (earth element), or white dedicated to the air element as many money-making and banking energies are done electronically

Timing: New moon, first quarter moon, Thursday at dawn, in a Jupiter or Venus planetary hour, first or second quarter moon in Taurus or Scorpio, or on a day when Venus or Jupiter is well aspected. The moon is exalted in the sign of Taurus; therefore, any day the moon is in Taurus and is well aspected (such as sextiles and trines) is an excellent time for any prosperity, money, or good fortune magick.

Note: To make lodestone oil, place one teaspoon of magnetic sand and seven lodestones in a jelly jar. Cover with sunflower oil or mineral oil. Place in a window facing east. Let set for three days. Remove lodestones, then strain and bottle oil.

Guardian Angel

Herbs: High John, lavender, marjoram, witchgrass, St. John's wort

Gemstone: Blue lace agate

Other Inclusions: Guardian angel prayer; frankincense and myrrh resins; winged charms; dirt, stones or flowers from a place that you feel is holy or spiritual

Magickal Oil: Frankincense, nag champa, sandalwood

Color Choices: Colors associated with angels can be a highly personal choice; go with your intuition

Timing: New moon; first quarter moon; full moon; Sunday, Monday, or Wednesday at dawn; in a sun planetary hour, in a moon planetary hour, or on a Mercury planetary hour

Protection

Herbs: Beth root, violet flowers, hydrangea flowers, clove, lavender

Gemstone: Smokey quartz

Other Inclusion: SATOR square, pentacle charm

Magickal Oil: Violet, gardenia, or other protection oil

Color Choices: Blue, black, white

Timing: New moon, full moon, Monday or Saturday at twilight or dusk, moon in Cancer, moon in Scorpio, moon in Taurus (protection of property), in a moon or Saturn planetary hour

Success

Herbs: Mint, Low John, sunflower, elecampane, buckeye, marigold

Gemstone: Red jasper

Other Inclusion: Magnet

Magickal Oil: Cedar, pine, or other success oil

Color Choices: Red, orange, yellow, purple, white

Timing: New or full moon; on a Sunday, Tuesday, or Thursday at noon; moon in Leo, moon in Taurus, or moon in Sagittarius OR the moon sign that fits the type of success that you desire (for example, if you wanted success in writing, you would pick the moon in Gemini or Sagittarius, being sure that there are no harsh aspects to the moon or other planets); planetary hour of the sun (success) or Mars (victory)

Divination

Herbs: Angelica, anise seed, celandine, mugwort, orange peel, myrrh

Gemstone: Hematite, moonstone, crystal, turquoise, blue tiger's-eye

Magickal Oil: Nag champa, patchouli, or other clarity or divination oil

Color Choices: Aqua, silver, light blue, purple, white

Timing: New moon, moon in Aquarius or Pisces, on a Monday at midnight, in the planetary hour of Mercury, or when Neptune is well aspected

Healing (General)

Herbs: Dogwood blossoms, black walnut, horehound, hyssop, celandine

Gemstone: Bloodstone, howlite

Magickal Oil: Combination of rose and dogwood, eucalyptus, or other healing oil

Color Choices: Green, pink, purple, white

Timing: New moon for promoting healing; third quarter moon for banishing illness; moon in Virgo or Cancer; planetary hour of the moon for healing; planetary hour of Saturn for banishing illness; dawn for healing; noon for general good health; twilight or midnight for banishing illness. When the moon is in Taurus, a poppet dedicated to the angel Haniel can facilitate healing for a broken heart or emotional pain.

Concentration

Herbs: Myrrh, spearmint, rosemary

Gemstone: Fluorite, hematite

Magickal Oil: Spearmint

Color Choices: Silver, blue, purple, white

Timing: New moon; first and second quarter moons; moon in Aquarius; Wednesday at dawn; planetary hour of Mercury. Gemini or Scorpio moon can also be used.

Lucky Lady

Herbs: Bergamot, mint, allspice, ginger, cinquefoil, honeysuckle leaves or root

Gemstone: Jade, calcite, amazonite, citrine

Magickal Oil: Orange, mint, or good luck oil

Other Inclusions: Magnet, lucky charms such as clover, dollar sign, etc.

Color Choices: Gold, red, purple, green

Timing: New moon, first and second quarter moons, Thursday at dawn or noon, planetary hour of the sun or Jupiter or when the sun or Jupiter are well aspected. Planetary hour of Venus (attraction) can also be used.

Good Marriage

Make poppets to represent the gender of the partners. After the poppets are completed, they should be ritually sewn together. If you are looking for a marriage partner, inclusions in the poppet should be a magnet and a written list of the qualities you desire in an ideal mate.

Herbs: Basil, orange peel, hazel leaves, ginseng, oak leaves, jasmine flowers

Gemstone: Rose quartz

Magickal Oil: A combination of rose and orange

Other Inclusions: An item from both individuals in the partnership—these items should be sealed together with glue or tied together with string

Color Choices: White, blue, gold, pink

Timing: New moon, first and second quarter moons, moon in Libra, on a Friday at dawn or noon, on a Sunday at dawn, planetary hour of the sun or Venus. Note: This timing is general.

Steady Income

Herbs: Devil's shoestring, cedar chips, cinquefoil, chamomile, yellow dock, snake root, galangal

Gemstone: Green aventurine, jade, moss agate, pearl

Other Inclusions: Gold, silver, or copper; dirt from a place that you know to be prosperous and matches the type of work that you do

Magickal Oil: A combination of honeysuckle, one drop of honey, and patchouli or a prosperity- or money-drawing magickal oil

Color Choices: Gold, purple

Timing: New moon, first and second quarter moons, full moon, on a Thursday or Friday at dawn or noon, moon in Taurus, moon in Scorpio (if your income is based on buying and selling), moon in Gemini or Aquarius (if your money comes from the internet). Planetary hours of Sun, Jupiter, Venus, or Mercury.

Catch a Thief

Herbs: Tobacco, black pepper, red pepper, nettle, patchouli, blackthorn

Gemstone: Tiger's-eye, bloodstone

Other Inclusions: Hard candy, spiderweb, hair net, mouse glue trap, grave dirt

Magickal Oil: An attraction oil, molasses, or honey

Color Choices: Black, gray, or white or a combination of red, white, and black

Timing: The Gemini moon is known for its energy flow to capture thieves and criminals and to bring back lost items. The magick is best done either at dawn, midnight, or 3:00 AM (the hour of dark magick). Other possible times for spellwork include new moon, dark moon, Wednesday at midnight or 3:00 AM (ruled by Mercury) or Saturday (same times). Use planetary hours of Saturn (limits) or Mercury.

"True Dat"/Truth

Herbs: Mint, horehound, rosemary, devil's shoestring

Gemstone: Tiger's-eye, iolite, calcite, kyanite

Other Inclusions: Spiderweb, hair net, mouse glue trap, gum chewed by the liar

Magickal Oil: Spearmint and devil's shoestring added to sunflower oil or jojoba carrier oil

Color Choices: White, purple

Timing: There are several astrological signs that lend themselves well to truth: Sagittarius, Libra, Gemini, Scorpio, and Aquarius; the moon in any of these signs may be of great assistance

Banish Nightmares or Destroy Illusions

Herbs: Nettle, yarrow, lavender, leek, larkspur

Gemstone: Peridot, snowflake obsidian, jet

Other Inclusions: Frankincense resin

Magickal Oil: Lavender or general banishing oil

Color Choices: Black, dark blue, lavender, gray, white

Timing: Moon in Aries can assist in banishing problems that have caused heartache, pain, or problems that have ventured into your sleep time. In a Pisces moon there is a greater connection to the astral realms. Banishments of all types are usually done on a third or fourth quarter moon, at dusk, at midnight or 3:00 AM, on a Saturday, or in the planetary hour of Saturn (drawing on the power of limits).

Remove Pain
Physical, Emotional, or Spiritual

Herbs: Hyssop, lavender

Gemstone: Amethyst, apache tears, botswana agate

Magickal Oil: Place willow bark, goldenseal, and kava-kava in a small bottle; add jojoba carrier oil (this is not for the body; it is only for magick)

Other Inclusions: Three small sticks cut from any tree at dawn—be sure to leave an offering

Color Choices: White

Action: Write a list of all things that are causing you pain and attach it to the outside of the dolly with twine. Burn the doll.

Timing: Moon in Cancer, Taurus, or Gemini. Moon in the third or fourth quarter. On a Monday, Wednesday, or Saturday. In a Mercury or Saturn planetary hour.

Release
Physical, Emotional, or Spiritual

Herbs: Salt, olive leaf, lemon verbena

Gemstone: None

Magickal Oil: Lavender, lemongrass

Color Choices: White

Action: Write a list of all things that you want to release and attach it to the outside of the dolly with twine. Spit on the doll. Burn the doll.

Timing: Moon in Cancer, Gemini, Capricorn, or Virgo. Moon in the third or fourth quarter. On a Monday, Wednesday, or Saturday. In a Mercury or Mars planetary hour.

"Evil, Begone"

Herbs: Wormwood, cinquefoil, black cumin, fava beans

Gemstone: Amethyst, black onyx, jet, obsidian combined with carnelian or red jasper

Magickal Oil: Frankincense, nag champa, sandalwood, or any of the three with hot pepper

Color Choices: Red, black, white

Timing: Aries, Sagittarius, or Scorpio moon. Third or further quarter. On a Tuesday or Saturday. In a Saturn or Mars planetary hour.

Reverse Harm

Herbs: Eucalyptus, red pepper, rue

Gemstone: Amethyst

Other Inclusions: Grave dirt, pins, nails, rubber band, picture of a boomerang

Magickal Oil: Eucalyptus or reversing oil

Color Choices: Black, white

Timing: Aries, Gemini, or Scorpio moon. Third or Fourth quarter moon. Tuesday, Wednesday, or Saturday at twilight, midnight, or 3:00 AM. Planetary hour of Mars, Mercury, or Saturn.

Stop Gossip

Herbs: Slippery elm, clove, lobelia, vetivert, pumpkin seeds, golden flax, devil's shoestring

Gemstone: Kyanite, emerald, jet, or amethyst

Magickal Oil: Clove, vetivert

Other Inclusions: Image of the ouroboros, pins or nails, picture of a rolled tongue

Color Choices: Purple, dark blue, gray

Timing: Aries, Gemini, or Scorpio moon. Third or fourth quarter moon. Tuesday, Wednesday, or Saturday at twilight, midnight, or 3:00 AM. Planetary hour of Mars, Mercury, or Saturn. An Aquarius moon can be helpful if this is an internet problem. Sagittarius moon if a legal problem. Use Capricorn moon if the structure around you is filled with gossip, libel, or slander (such as a group of people in an organization or on the job).

Travel Protection

Herbs: Juniper berries, basil, birch, comfrey, mugwort

Gemstone: Garnet, jet, aquamarine, moonstone

Other Inclusions: Charm of a horse or bird, or a picture of Sleipnir (Odin's eight-legged horse), silver wheel

Magickal Oil: Gardenia, violet

Color Choices: Blue, purple, white

Timing: Moon in Gemini, Sagittarius, or Cancer (all three signs are associated with travel or personal protection). Short distance—Gemini; long distance—Sagittarius. On a Monday, new moon, or full moon. Monday or Wednesday at dawn. Moon, Sun, or Mercury planetary hour.

Hex Breaker

Herbs: Vetivert, lime peel, devil's shoestring, witch grass, bamboo, galangal, chili pepper, wintergreen

Gemstone: Amethyst

Other Inclusions: Grave dirt, picture of a hammer, broken pottery

Magickal Oil: Lilac, wintergreen

Color Choices: Black, purple

Timing: Aries, Gemini, or Scorpio moon. Third or fourth quarter moon. Tuesday, Wednesday, or Saturday. Planetary hour of Mars, Mercury, or Saturn.

Funeral Guardian

The funeral guardian spirit doll travels with the deceased into the afterlife. It can be placed in the coffin, burned with the body during legal cremation, or burned afterwards if you are unable to put the doll with the body. If you can't get it in the coffin, you may be able to slip it into the grave. These dolls act as friends, companions, and servants for the deceased. They can be named or unnamed. They can be in human or animal form. If there is no time to construct a doll, buy a stuffed animal, make a slit in it, and put in a paper that says:

> *Come alive, O my friend, and guard my loved one (person or animal's name) night and day to the end of eternity. Bring him/her love, joy, and laughter. Ensure that he/she always walks in the light of love. So mote it be!*

Repeat this charm (or one like it) three times and quickly close the stuffed animal.

Herbs: Favorite herbs of the deceased or frankincense, nag champa, sandalwood

Gemstone: Crystal

Other Inclusions: Guardian angel prayer; frankincense and myrrh resins; winged charms; dirt, stones, or flowers from a place that you feel is holy or spiritual; a prayer to Anubis dressed in white rum

Magickal Oil: Frankincense, nag champa, sandalwood

Color Choices: The deceased's favorite color or white

Timing: If the death was unexpected, whenever you make the doll will be okay. If you have time or want to make dolls ahead as sympathy gifts when the time is right, use the new moon, first quarter moon, or full moon; Sunday, Monday, or Wednesday at dawn; in a sun planetary hour, in a moon planetary hour, or on a Mercury planetary hour.

eight

POPPET PATTERNS

Everything has a pattern. Each pattern is made of energy threads (see them as sticky, if you like) that upon repetition unfold into manifestation, whether we are talking about joy, a bird, illness, or a rock. Each thread has a vibration that when matched with others creates the symphony of the thing.

The beginning is quick (that which you cannot see) but may not be long lasting. The more the repetition, the greater the chance of birth into what we desire. Every diversion from our initial vibration dissolves the original amorphous blueprint and begins a new pattern. Repetition with purity may ensure the replication of the thread, which creates the pattern, which makes the thing—moss, fire, an elephant, or wisdom.

Everything is thread.

Everything is a pattern.

Everything sings into existence.

The universe is a tapestry of energy in which you are a creator/creatrix.

It truly is within your hands.

Whether it be a thought or an action, if you begin any birth process with love in your heart and a single focus of intent, the unfoldment can move forward unhindered and the chances of birth are much greater.

You can't say "I must love this" and force yourself to do so. Instead, this love is an unfolding of compassion, where there is no judgement, just the desire to create, to bring joy, or to heal.

The following patterns were constructed in this way: a single thread, replicated on the platform of compassion, delivered without judgment to you for the ultimate manifestation.

Remember that you can adjust the sizing of any of these patterns.

SIMPLE MALE

SIMPLE FEMALE

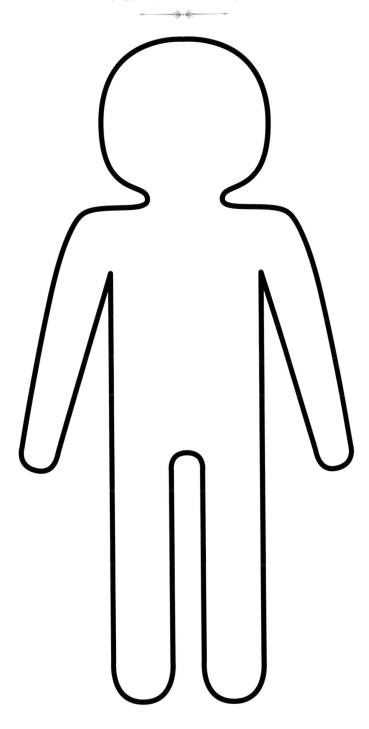

INTERMEDIATE MALE

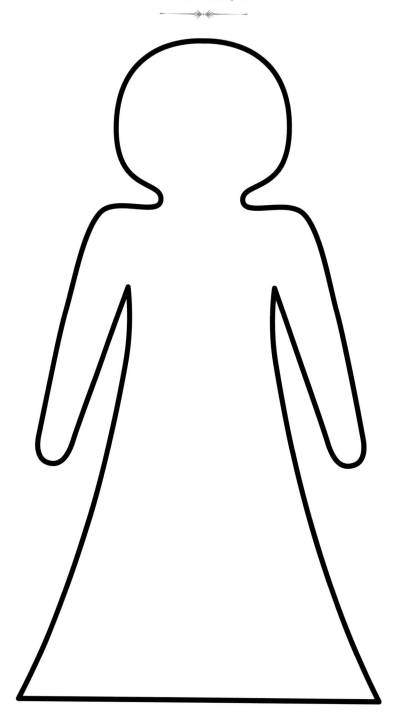

INTERMEDIATE FEMALE

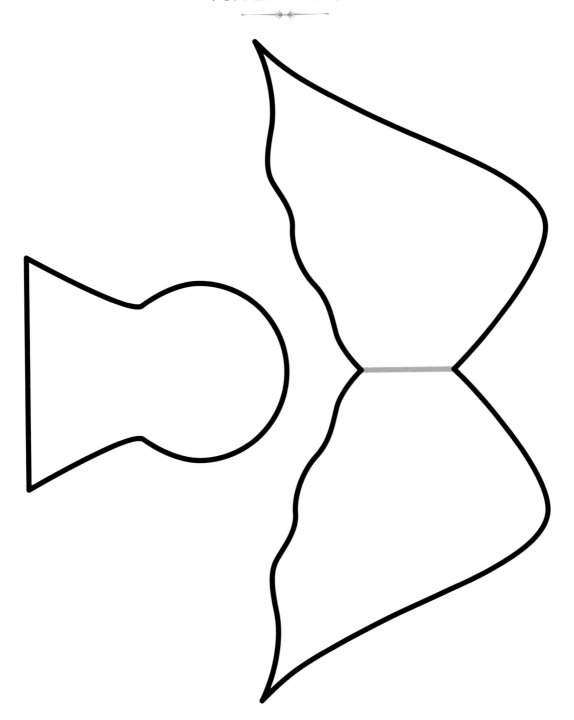

WINGS & LITTLE SPIRIT

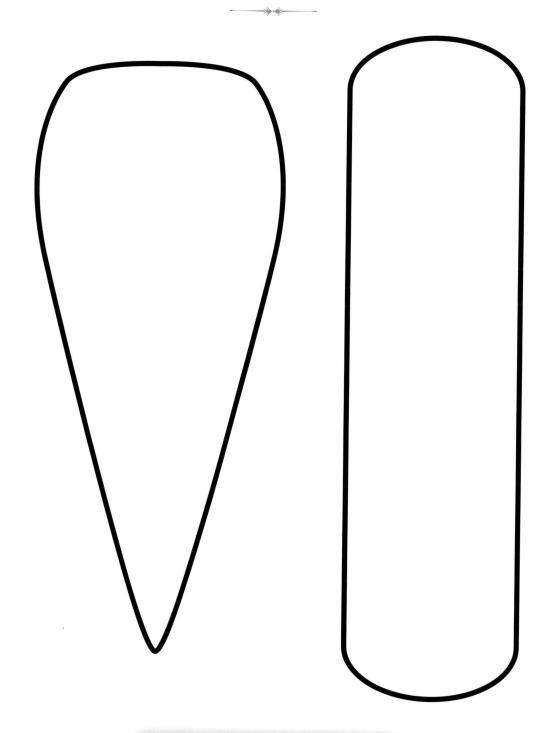

TEARDROP & ROUNDED RECTANGLE

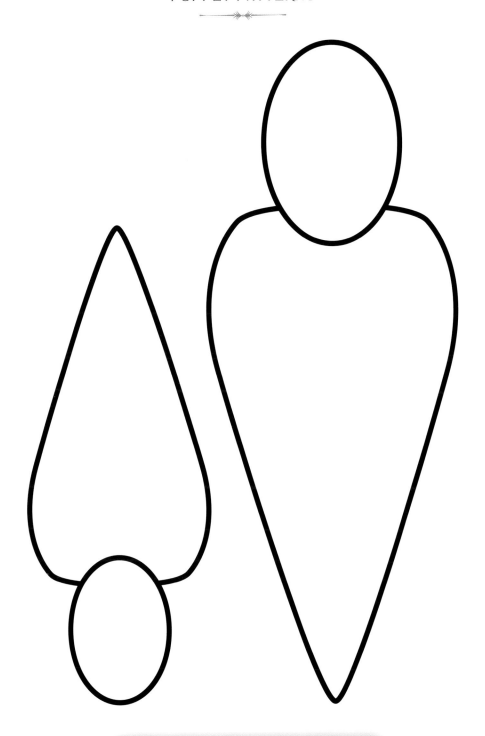

NO ARMS TEARDROP

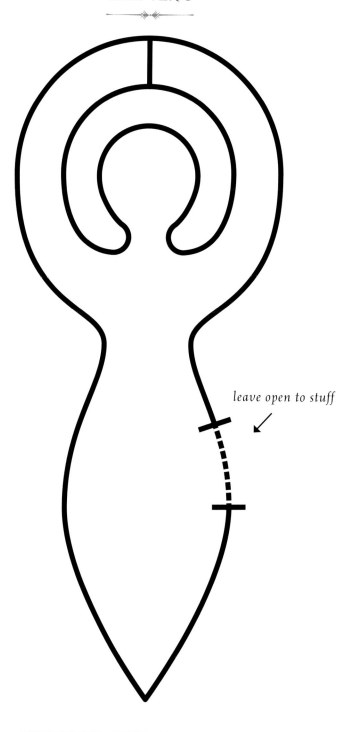

leave open to stuff

GODDESS

THREE-HEADED

For top, cut one out of a single piece of fabric.
For skirt, fold fabric, lay pattern on fold, and cut one.

Fold this edge over, press, and stitch using a ½-inch seam.

For skirt, place this edge on fold.

DREAMING POPPET SKIRT & SHIRT

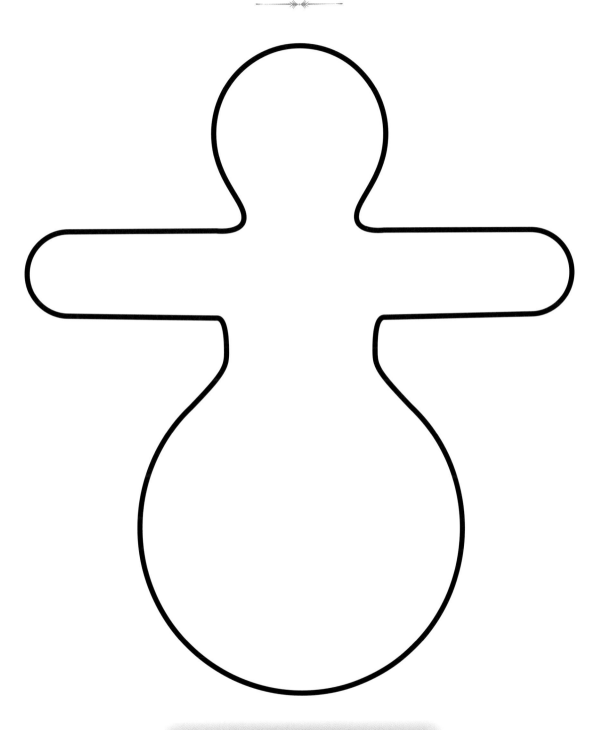

SPIRIT DOLLY ONE

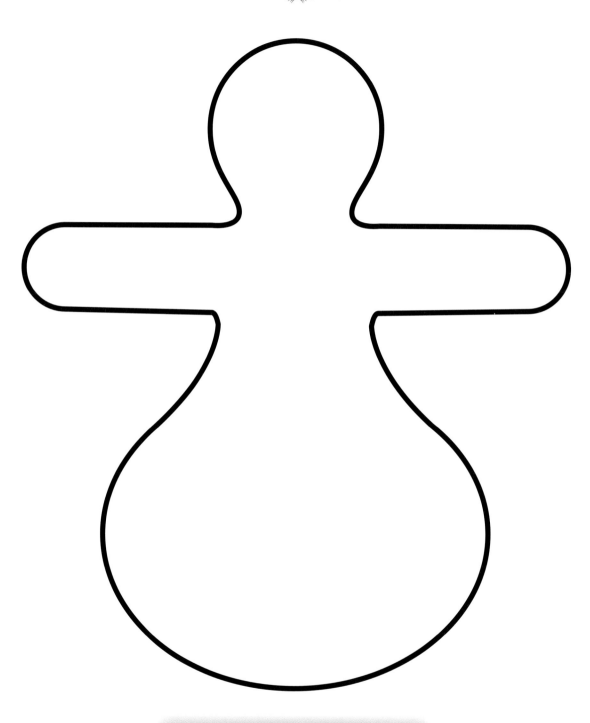

SPIRIT DOLLY TWO

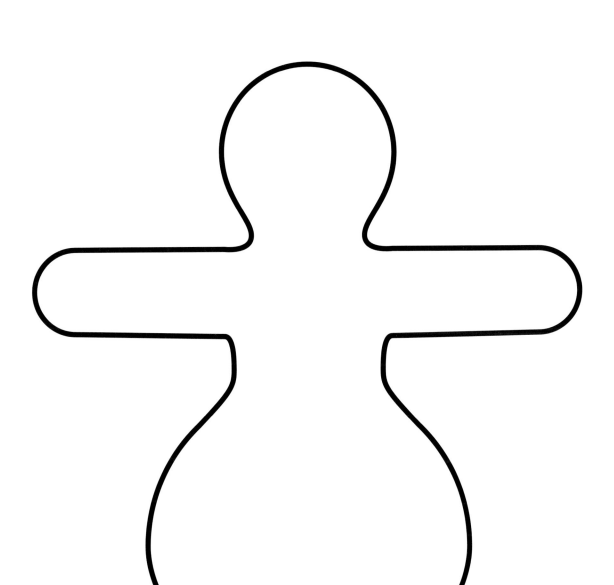

SPIRIT DOLLY THREE

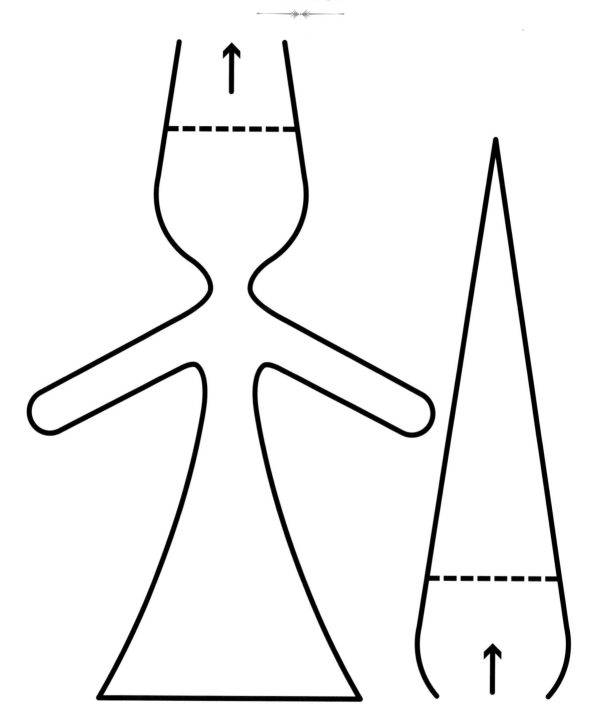

SALT DOLLY-DO

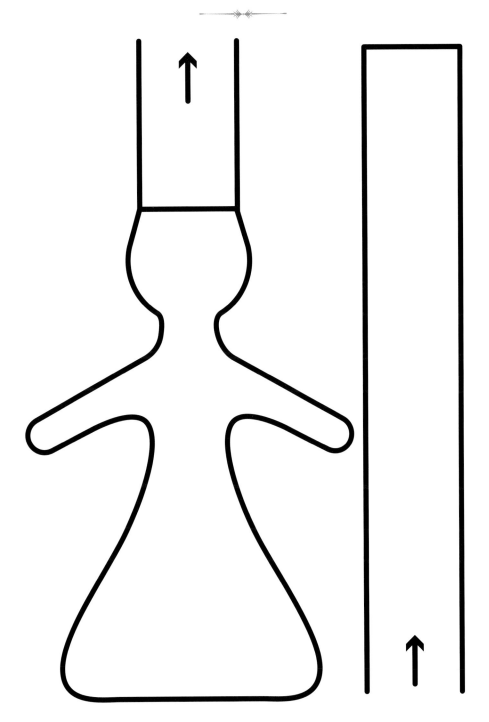

SUSIE SALT HEALER'S TOOL

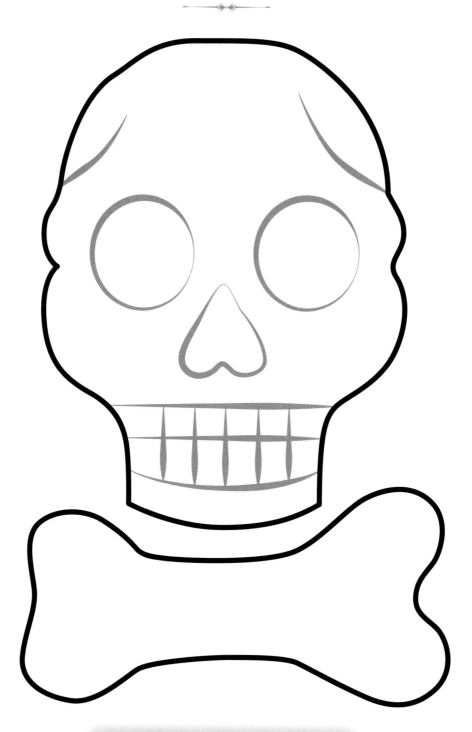

BASKET OF BONES ORNIES

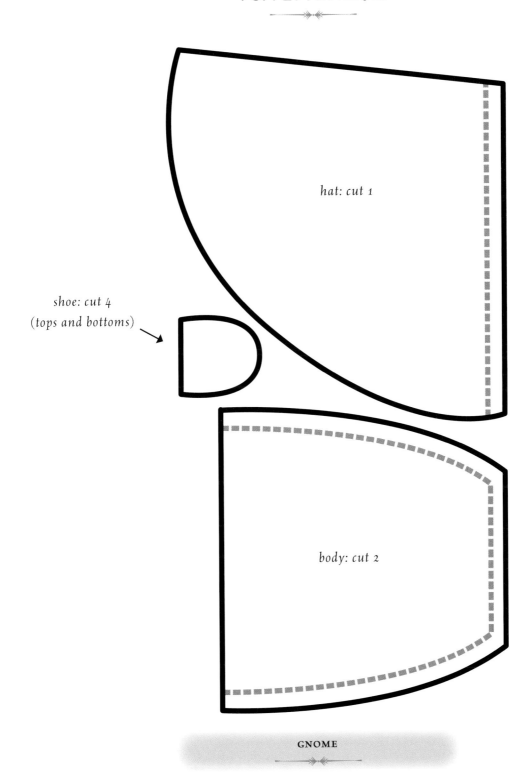

hat: cut 1

shoe: cut 4
(tops and bottoms)

body: cut 2

GNOME

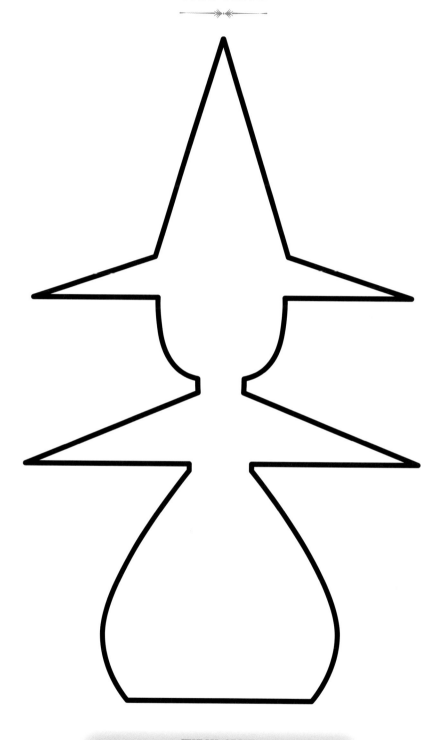

WITCH OPPIT

CHAKRA OPPIT

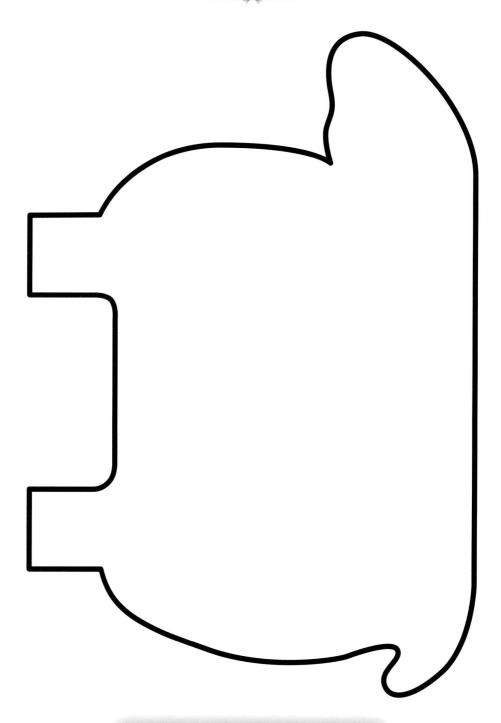

ADULT SHEEP

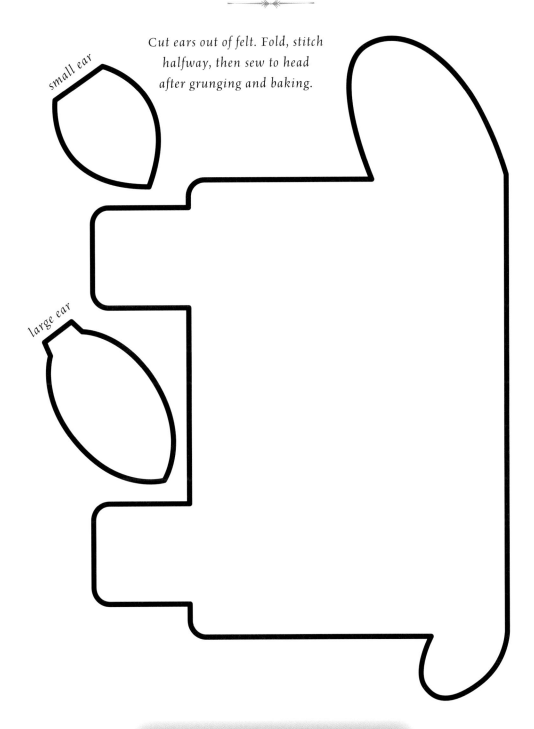

small ear

large ear

Cut ears out of felt. Fold, stitch halfway, then sew to head after grunging and baking.

SHEEP ORNIE

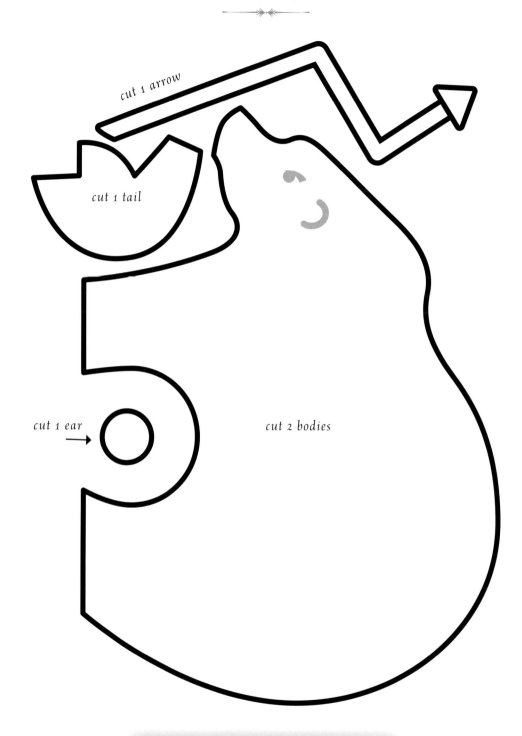

cut 1 arrow

cut 1 tail

cut 1 ear →

cut 2 bodies

MEDICINE BEAR

cut 4 ears

cut 2
bodies and tails

stuff tail before sewing into body seam

Ears: sew wrong sides together,
leaving bottom open. Turn and
stuff with fiberfill stuffing, then
sew closed. Insert pipe cleaners
if you want ears to bend.

GOOD FORTUNE MAGICK CAT

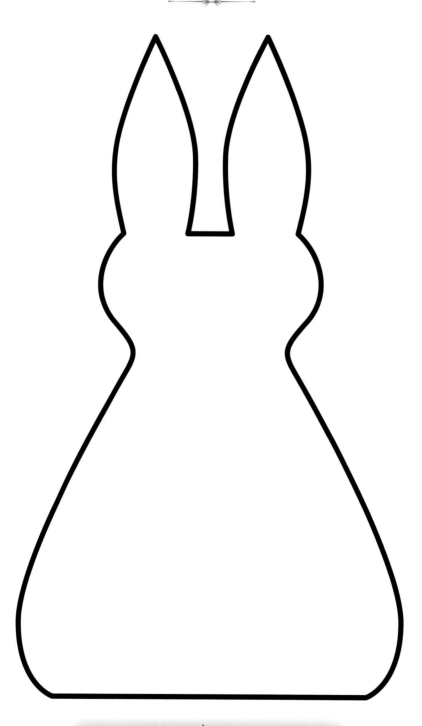

BRIGID'S BUNNY

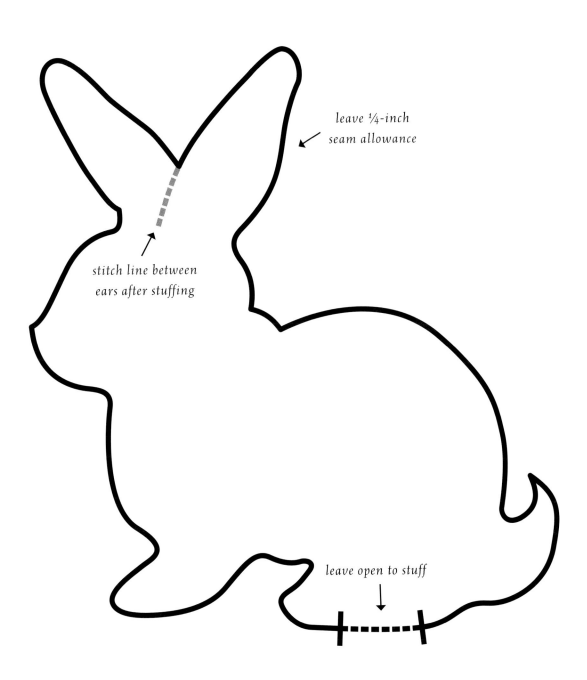

leave ¼-inch
seam allowance

stitch line between
ears after stuffing

leave open to stuff

BUNNIE ORNIE

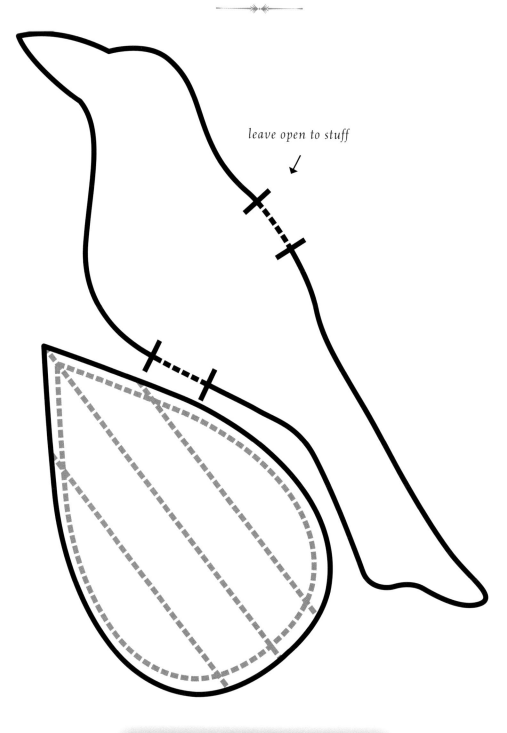

leave open to stuff

BIRD PRIM

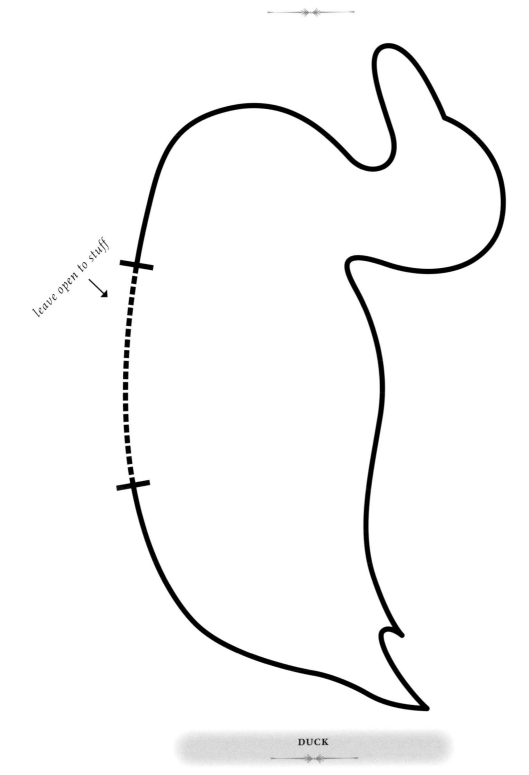

leave open to stuff

DUCK

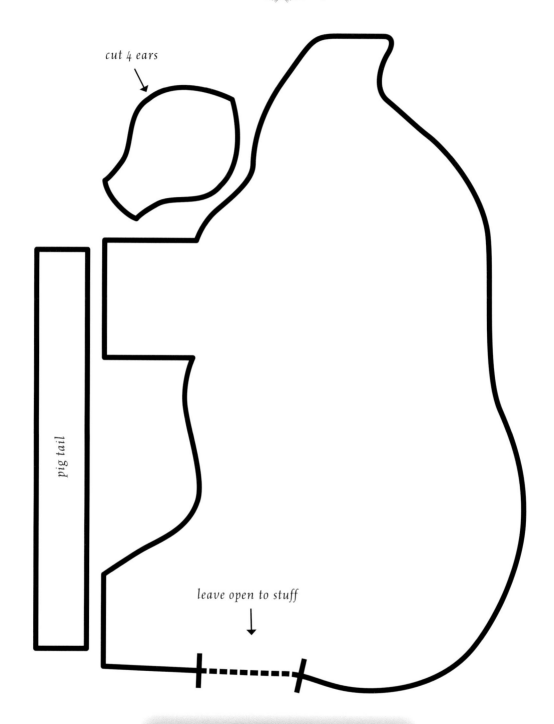

cut 4 ears

pig tail

leave open to stuff

PROSPERITY PIG

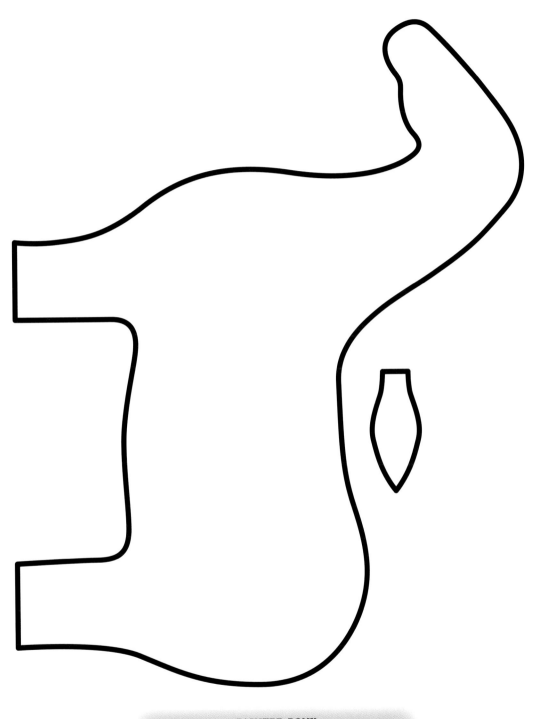

PAINTED PONY

⟩⟩⟨⟨

cut 4 wings

SWAN ORNIE

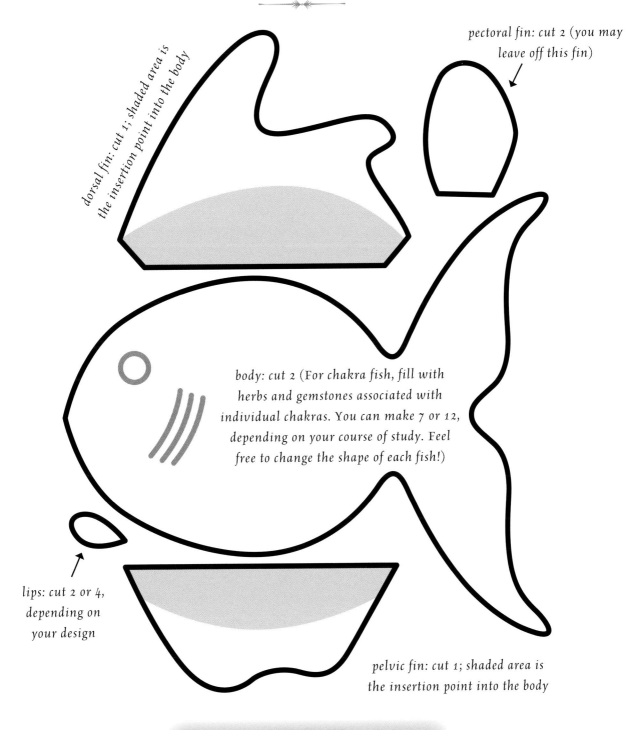

pectoral fin: cut 2 (you may leave off this fin)

dorsal fin: cut 1; shaded area is the insertion point into the body

body: cut 2 (For chakra fish, fill with herbs and gemstones associated with individual chakras. You can make 7 or 12, depending on your course of study. Feel free to change the shape of each fish!)

lips: cut 2 or 4, depending on your design

pelvic fin: cut 1; shaded area is the insertion point into the body

CHAKRA FISH

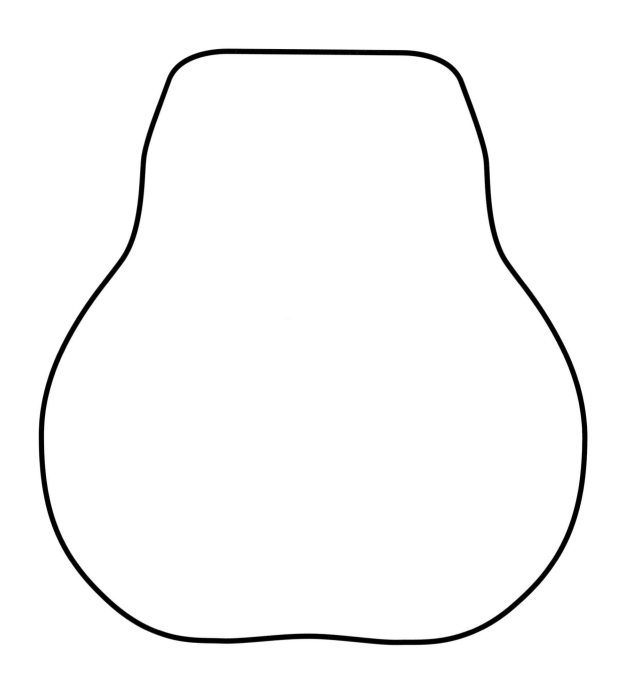

TACO CAT

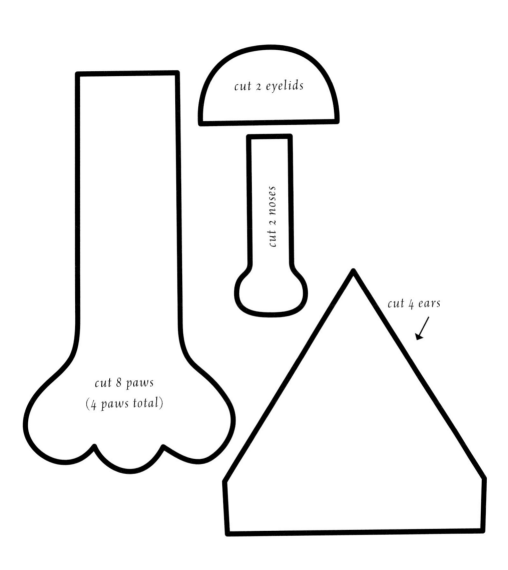

cut 2 eyelids

cut 2 noses

cut 4 ears

cut 8 paws
(4 paws total)

TACO CAT FIXINGS

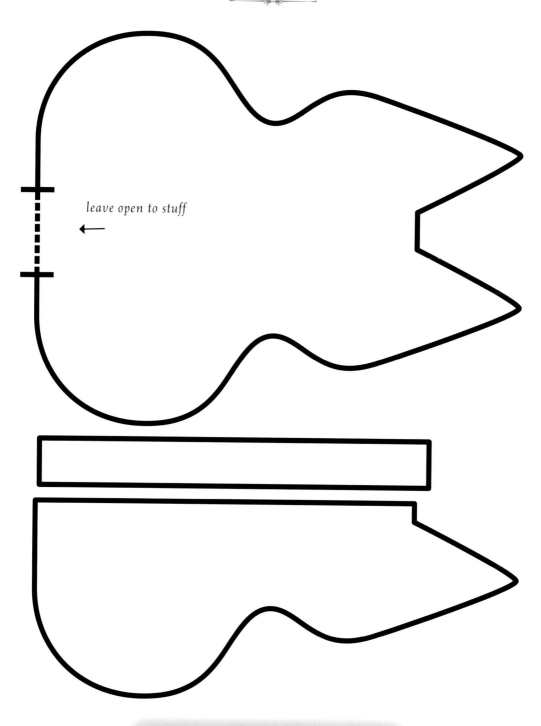

leave open to stuff

KITTEN PRIM

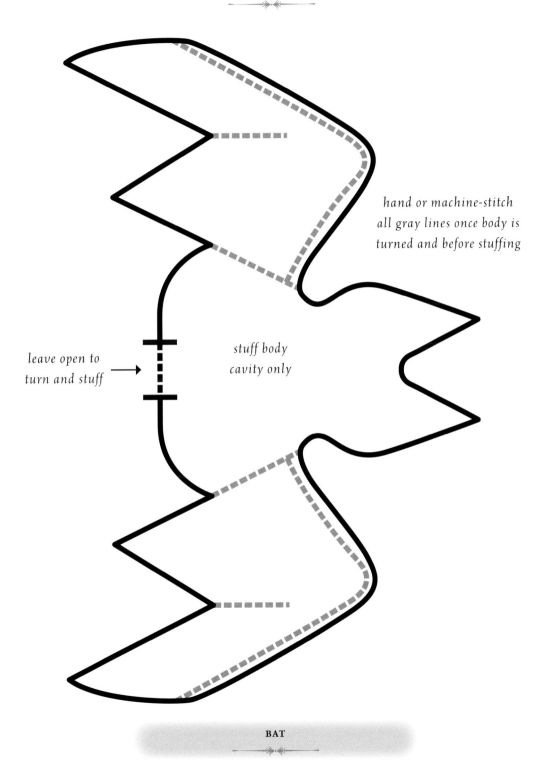

hand or machine-stitch
all gray lines once body is
turned and before stuffing

leave open to
turn and stuff

stuff body
cavity only

BAT

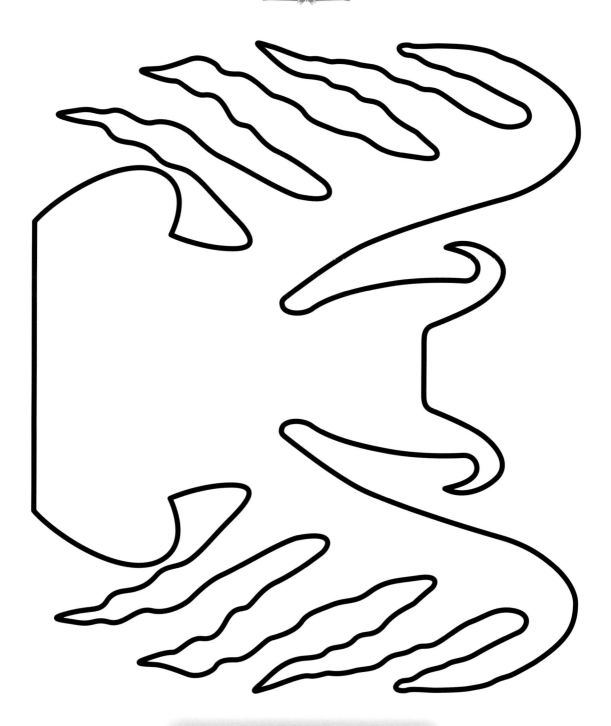

GARGOYLE

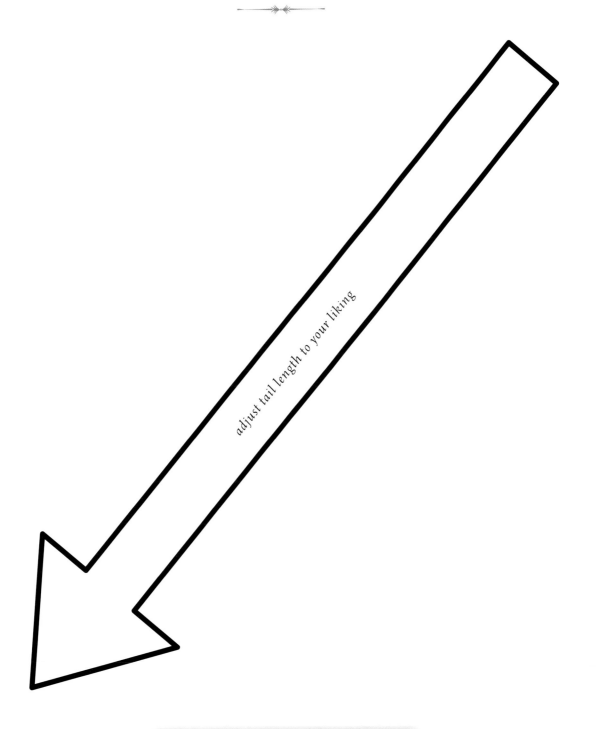

adjust tail length to your liking

GARGOYLE TAIL

epilogue

To Create *is* To Change

Every practitioner is different, relying on experience, training, practice, belief, and crafting ability. The poppets, dollies, and enchanted animals herein are merely a reflection of my work; how you choose to construct and empower your projects is entirely up to you. Be creative. Embrace change. Be daring! Let your passion and your intuition be your guides.

I would like to thank you for purchasing this book and working along with me. It is my greatest desire that this information brings you ultimate joy! Don't stop with what I've given here; follow your heart. Large or small, plain or highly decorated, your poppets, spirit dolls, and magickal animals will be delighted to assist you in changing your world. Just ask them!

Your enchanted dolls, poppets, and spirit animals become patterns of being in their own right, and in that blending of energy through fabric, thread, paper, and stuffing to make the unique design, the vibration may call for additional items, whether purposeful or whimsical, that you feel you must include. It doesn't matter what you choose, as the importance is a piece of the totality. These choices are extremely intuitive. No one can tell you the "right" formula; only you know this. As you stand in your experience—your schooling, your knowledge, your events and emotions—only you can be the creator or creatrix of the work that you do.

There is no mass production. There is no right way (other than we don't want our doll to fall apart—or maybe we do). Sometimes our dolls will tell us that they want a special blanket or a bag to hold more charms—something that can only be included after the doll has been completed. Perhaps the doll wishes to sit in a bag as part of its personal protection or would like to travel with you in a special bag. Sometimes the doll will call for a companion; for example, I finished a large pumpkin doll who implicitly told me that she had to have a friend with her. Might I make a raven? So I did—Priscilla the Pumpkin now has Peabody the Raven sitting on her arm.

In the beginning, I felt that listening to these thoughts was stupid. And, to be honest, people even called me stupid. I remember reading on social media someone's opinion on how dumb I was as they laughed at my country prim dolls and animals. There I was, following my passion, and someone felt the need to publicly diss my bliss. And then I realized—don't buy into someone's agony. It isn't yours. It doesn't belong to you. All these people are doing is telling the world they are in pain, and then trying to mask their own problems with voluminous prose of feigned outrage based on this cause or that—the smoke and mirrors of psychological dysfunction. It wasn't about me at all, not one little bit. Rather than fuss about it any further, I chose to look forward. To concentrate on joy. To settle for nothing less than healing.

You may have noticed that this topic of conversation flows through the pages of this book. I have been asked often lately about being bullied and how to magickally handle it, especially on the internet in regard to one's creative product, whether you are writing or drawing or making little stuffed animals. Our electronic age, as marvelous as it might be, has sacrificed much in the realms of positive communication. Once upon a time it was only the famous who were forced to deal with negativity through the media; now, with the internet, everyone is fair game.

My advice?

Go ahead: make the poppet.

Or the drawing.

Or the new dance move.

Or whatever your little creative heart desires.

For in art lies joy and healing for all.

May the power of the dollies be ever with you!

Silver Raven Wolf
APRIL 2017

Bibliography

Bardon, Franz. *Initiation into Hermetics: The Path of the True Adept.* Salt Lake City, UT: Merkur Publishing, 1956.

Bennett, Hal Zina. 1993. *Zuni Fetishes: Using Native American Objects for Meditation, Reflection, and Insight.* New York: HarperCollins, 1993.

Bromberg, Erik. *The Hopi Approach to the Art of Kachina Doll Carving.* Atglen, PA: Schiffer Publishing, 1986.

Colton, Harold S. *Hopi Kachina Dolls with a Key to Their Identification.* Albuquerque, NM: University of New Mexico Press, 1949.

Deveney, John Patrick. *Paschal Beverly Randolph: A Nineteenth-Century Black American Spiritualist, Rosicrucian, and Sex Magician.* Albany, NY: State University of New York Press, 1997.

Edward, Linda. *Cloth Dolls from Ancient to Modern: A Collector's Guide.* Atglen, PA: Schiffer Publishing, 1997.

Faraone, Christopher, and Dirk Obbink. *Magika Hiera: Ancient Greek Magic & Religion.* New York: Oxford University Press, 1991.

Greer, John Michael, and Christopher Warnock. *The Picatrix.* Adocentyn Press, 2010.

Lake-Thom, Bobby. *Spirits of the Earth: A Guide to Native American Nature Symbols, Stories, and Ceremonies.* New York: Penguin Books, 1997.

Lasansky, Jeanette. *Bits and Pieces Textile Traditions.* University of Pennsylvania Press, 1991.

Lecouteux, Claude. *The Book of Grimoires: The Secret Grammar of Magic.* Rochester, VT: Inner Traditions, 2002.

Leek, Sybil. *Cast Your Own Spell.* New York: Pinnacle Books, 1970.

Magnus, Albertus. *Egyptian Secrets of Albertus Magnus, or White and Black Art for Man and Beast.* No publisher listed.

Peterson, Joseph. *The Sixth and Seventh Books of Moses.* Lake Worth, FL: Ibis Press, 2008.

Pinch, Geraldine. *Magick in Ancient Egypt.* Austin, TX: University of Texas Press, 1994.

Randolph, Paschal Beverly, and Maria de Naglowska. *Magia Sexualis.* Rochester, VT: Inner Traditions, 1931.

Glossary

You will not find these definitions on the internet—they were constructed as an aid to working through this book and are relative only to the material herein.

Braucherei/Pow-Wow: Pennsylvania German folk magickal practices, which are a combination of German High Magick, Nordic pre-Christian practices, Southern country philosophy, American Gothic rural folk magick, Gypsy influence and Native American herbal cures for the ailments of human and beast, the seen and unseen, medicinal and…otherwise. Pow-Wow is a unique system that relies on one's belief, intent, and the manipulation of energy by means of what we now understand to be the quantum physics of the mind. The system of Braucherei/Pow-Wow works regardless of the practitioner's preference in religion because of its simple and powerful foundation: belief.

Granny Magick: Folk magick practices, beliefs, and superstitions of early Americana, particularly along the Appalachian Trail, but not limited to there.

Ornies: Small (3 to 6 inches) stitched ornaments made of felt, fabric, and some type of stuffing, and often displayed in bowls—these items are sometimes called bowl ornaments or tucks.

Poppet: A poppet is any doll that represents a human being, real or imagined.

Primitive Dolls: Folk art style of early Americana; however, primitive doll styles can be found in all cultures throughout history. Designs were considered "unskilled" or rough-hewn due to materials, skill, or primitive implements used.

Prims: The definition today is difficult, as the art world and consumer taste continues to change, adding new words or reinventing old words at fad speed. Today, prim means a design that is a throwback to an earlier, more rustic era (which era is debatable). Prims are simple, unsophisticated, unrefined. Prims can also be considered American Gothic, particularly the animal designs. Many of the animals in this book are considered prims—the bowl of kitties, the ducks, or any animal that is grunged or looks primitive.

Shelf-Sitter: A handmade ornament, design, or animal constructed of fabric that sits on a shelf and most likely needs to be propped for display.

Spirit Doll: A spirit doll is any doll that represents a particular energy or group of blended energies created and then released for whatever purpose you desire. Spirit dolls can be in the shape of people or any image you wish. The point is that the design of the dolls speaks to the heart of the matter—that in your mind the spirit doll absolutely represents a specific collection of energy that can be as single-purposed as joy or as complicated as the desire to succeed in a particular line of business, where several steps and associations are required. The energy can be the magnification of a single astrological planet or the strength of a vibrational color or a blend. A spirit doll carries the energy to the target; a poppet *is* the target.

Tucks: Small (3 to 6 inches) handmade ornaments that can be "tucked" in a corner for decoration, on a shelf, in a basket, etc. Tucks and ornies are basically the same things.

Whisper Magick: Folk magickal practice with a Braucherei/Pow-Wow foundation and added Granny Magick techniques. The main premise is the whispering of chants, charms, and prayers to manipulate the world around you in positive ways. This particular magickal study includes plant and animal nature balance, utilizing what you already have on hand, and making your own supplies.

Index